. . . so they understand . . .

Cultural Issues in Oral History

Photo by Karen Brewster, July, 1996.

"In between the lines is something special going on in
their minds, and that has got to be brought to light,
so they understand just exactly what is said."

—Chief Peter John, June, 1999

. . . so they understand . . .
Cultural Issues in Oral History

William Schneider

Documentation, Representation, Preservation, and Interpretation
Illustrated with Stories from South Africa, Alaska, and the Yukon

UTAH STATE UNIVERSITY PRESS
Logan, Utah

Utah State University Press
Logan, Utah

All royalties, after expenses, from the sale of this book will be donated to support the Alaska Native Studies Program at the University of Alaska Fairbanks.

Cover design: Richard Howe.
Front cover illustrations: *Top left,* Chief Peter John; photo by Karen Brewster. *Top right, left to right,* Christian Tritt, Sarah Frank, Dan Frank, Abraham Christian. *Right,* Mamabola elders, *left to right,* M. Mogashoa, J. M. V. Mogashoa, R. Chueu. *Bottom left,* Herschel Island Cultural Study participants, *left to right,* Renie Arey, Murielle Nagy, Dora Malegana, Jean Tardiff, Kathleen Hansen, and Sarah Meyook; photo courtesy of the Yukon Heritage Branch and the Inuvialuit Regional Corporation.
Back cover illustrations: *Top right,* Howard Luke; photo by Bill Burke. *Bottom left,* Phegello "Zakes" Letshela in front of the National Library of South Africa.

Manufactured in the United States of America
Printed on acid-free paper

Library of Congress Cataloging-in-Publication Data

Schneider, William.
   So they understand : cultural issues in oral history / William Schneider.
      p. cm.
"Documentation, representation, preservation, and interpretation, illustrated with stories from South Africa, Alaska, and the Yukon."
Includes bibliographical references.
   ISBN 0-87421-550-1 (pbk. : alk. paper)
   1. Oral tradition. 2. Oral history. I. Title.
   GR72 .S35 2002

Contents

Illustrations

Acknowledgments

Compiling acknowledgments is a reminder that for me, it is the people and their contributions that make this work possible and rewarding. In the spirit of *ubuntu*, I want to recognize the following people.

Earlier drafts of this work were read by Margaret Blackman, John Miles Foley, Ray Barnhardt, Jim Magdanz, Don Ritchie, Thoko Hlatywayo, Murielle Nagy, Zakes Letshela, Verne Harris, Linda Johnson, David Krupa, and students in my classes at the University of Alaska Fairbanks. Thank you to all of them for useful comments; I know that this work is better because of their reviews.

I appreciate help received from Sello Hatang in locating materials on Nelson Mandela, Ethel Kriger for discussions of ubuntu and other traditional phrases, Thoko Hlatywayo for numerous conversations to clarify meanings of interviews conducted at the University of the North, and Ken Frank for identification of people from Venetie village in Interior Alaska.

I had good editorial help from Sue Mitchell here in Fairbanks and on-going support from John Alley at Utah State University Press. I can't think of a more supportive editor. I also appreciate Jennifer Collier's help as I worked through contracting details.

I appreciate assistance I had from Bill Burke, Dave Libbey, Karen Brewster, Bob Betts, Dave Nelson, Richard Veazey, Kim Armstrong, Shannon Olson, the Inuvialuit Regional Corporation, Yukon Heritage, Linda Johnson, Roger Kaye, Murielle Nagy, and Molly Lee in identifying and obtaining photos.

I realize that this work would not have been possible without the support of the Rasmuson Library permanent staff, in particular Robyn Russell, who has managed the oral history collection with a library professional's attention to detail and accountability. Appendix B is her work. The library permitted me to take a sabbatical leave during the 1997 year, and a Fulbright Scholarship gave me the chance to work in South Africa and to learn more about oral narrative. Paul

McCarthy, library director, supported my travel back to South Africa this past summer, and an earlier trip was supported by the National Archives of South Africa and the University of Witwatersrand. These trips deepened my understanding of South Africans and the way oral narrative plays a part in their lives.

Many of the advancements in the way we do oral history recordings and the way we represent them electronically through the computer came from talented people who helped make the Project Jukebox dream come true. I want to acknowledge Felix Vogt, Dan Grahek, Mary Larson, David Krupa, Karen Brewster, Jarrod Decker, Bill Burke, Marla Bryson, and Cal White. Karen has been our key person tracking developments in electronic delivery of oral history on the Web, and her attention to ethical and legal issues is reflected in appendix C, a document she prepared.

Finally, thanks to my family—my wife, Sidney, and my daughter, Willa—for their support. And for patience over my lifetime, thanks to my mother, Harriet. who recently said, "I'm saying prayers it will get done in my lifetime . . . I get older and older."

Thank you all.

part one

How Stories Work

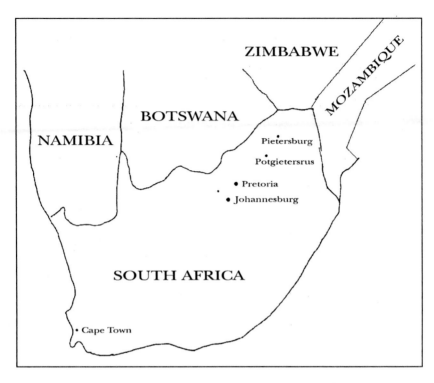

ZIMBABWE

MOZAMBIQUE

BOTSWANA

NAMIBIA

Pietersburg

Potgietersrus

• Pretoria

• Johannesburg

SOUTH AFRICA

• Cape Town

Barrow

Herschel Island

Inuvik

Kotzebue

Beaver

YUKON

Nome

Fairbanks

• Dawson

ALASKA

• Whitehorse

Anchorage

Sitka

Kodiak

Unalaska

Introduction

The setting is northern South Africa at graduation ceremonies for the University of the North (UNIN) in the fall of 1997. The university's red brick buildings stand out against the parched fields and modest homes. Beyond the fence and entry gates, cows and donkeys graze. This is an economically poor part of the country, and this university was designed and built during the years of apartheid to educate the people of the region.[1] Little did the authorities know that this place would become a center for resistance to the government, a place where many of today's leaders would gather to rally support for change. During those years police intervention was common and students were jailed. UNIN has not recovered from the revolution; students still agitate for change; boycott and protest are often the first and only course of action.

The chancellor of the university is Nelson Mandela, who at that time was the president of South Africa. President Mandela has come to the campus to meet with the administration and faculty, to confer the degrees at graduation, and to address the graduates and their families. He is a tall, dignified looking man, and his warmth and interest in the people is evident. As he makes his way down the aisle to the stage, he stops frequently to greet and reach out to the older people and the young children. On the stage, he looks out into the auditorium of excited guests, elders, parents, and young children. He shakes hands with each graduate and offers his personal congratulations.

But now, he has completed his formal remarks, removed his reading glasses and begins a story. I am situated with other faculty behind him on the stage, and it is a bit hard to hear his comments, so in this recalling, I rely on a video made of the speech by the UNIN Media Department. The audio quality is poor so I will quote as best I can and edit heavily where it is not possible to distinguish his words.

Perhaps let me have the humility of saying that, in my younger days, I, myself, was a destroyer. I was once sent to go and break a

3

meeting of the Communist Party. . . . It was a classic speech of a wise man, of a hero who analyzed the position of our people with an outline [of] how we can mobilize one another . . . or mobilize the entire country and how to overcome oppression . . . on us. That address was punctuated by prolonged ovation because it was a good speaker and he was making sense.

And the question was, what was I going to do? How was I going to carry out the task when people have you so filled with what they want to say? And I decided on a simple strategy and I said, "South Africa is like a big kraal. There are two bulls, one white coming from overseas, from a foreign country. There is a black bull produced by our soil. [Some] say the white bull must move in the kraal. I say the black bull from our own soil, the bull of [mentions three regions or chiefs]. I say that bull should lose [the white one]. What do you say?"

The same people that were cheering for [the speaker] were now cheering for me and I was able to break up the meeting. I had said nothing. [At this point the UNIN audience like the earlier audience was cheering for the black bull. Mandela quickly corrected them.] . . . No vision but that slogan. Now, when there are tensions, it is . . . your duty as people who do not fear opposition, who do not fear, . . . to identify good men and women in all communities amongst Africans, Colored, Indians, Whites, among the various political organizations. It doesn't matter which political organization they come [from]; there are good men and women. Your duty, especially young people, is to say, why are we fighting? . . . Why should we, when we have the opportunity of arming ourselves, why must we speak different voices?

You should be able to say why should the so-called leaders of political organizations destroy your own future . . .

Be positive, be constructive, and make sure that in every crisis the people of South Africa should emerge more united, more solid, and speaking with one voice. That is the homework I give you.

President Mandela's speech includes what may be an old story (the two bulls) retold within the larger story of how he broke up the Communist Party meeting. Most people there, and those who listen to the videotape, would say that he was imploring the audience to work together for South Africa, for the common good. He was telling us not to discriminate based on racial, ethnic, or political lines, that the greater good could be reached by everyone speaking with one voice.

That's probably all that I am qualified to report on, but I am quite sure that is not all that he was saying. Let me try to peel back some layers with your full understanding that I am raising questions more than speaking with authority. First there is the setting, UNIN, a university that has experienced year after year of unrest and disruption. This is a place that has a proud history of helping to cultivate the revolution that led to the new South Africa, but a place that is also struggling in the post-apartheid era to make the transition from revolutionary to democratic means to enact change. Nelson Mandela represents that change and is a living example of how to make the transition. This is further corroborated by his admittance that he didn't always make the right decision: "Perhaps let me have the humility of saying that, in my younger days, I, myself, was a destroyer."

I think Mandela was speaking directly to members of the UNIN community and calling for them to rely on reason and to work together. I suspect he knew that there had been long periods during the past year when the university was closed down to avoid violence, times when students closed the library and scared fellow students to keep them from attending classes.

You might know what he meant in his speech without knowing the history of UNIN, but would you know why he chose to say what he did on that occasion? I don't think he ever referred specifically to the university by name, but it sure felt like he was specifically speaking to us.

Then there is the story within the story—the two bulls in the kraal. He refers to it as a slogan, which would indicate that this story has a history of general use, that it is commonly understood. I am searching for that understanding and, like Joseph Sheppherd's research with the Ntumu people in the Cameroon (1988), I am reminded just how difficult it is to interpret sayings, adages, and riddles without an adequate knowledge of the oral traditions that inform them. In Mandela's story we might think that the two bulls should learn to get along, to use their joint might to plow the field, instead of fighting in the kraal. But to a farmer, this is ridiculous. My colleague at UNIN, Segothe Mokgoats'ana, in his manuscript, "It is herstory too," references the adage *Ga go na poo pedi ka sakeng*, which he interprets to mean, "There are no two bulls in the kraal." This reference is imbedded in his discussion of a "folk custom" that says a community has only one authority. The adage has also been used in the academic arena. Carolyn Hamilton, in her commentary on my use of the Mandela speech, noted that the expression was used recently at the University of Witwatersrand to describe a power struggle between two Western-educated African academics, one Black and one White.[2]

So, how are we to understand Mandela's use of the story? Is he saying we should not be like two bulls in a kraal, that we should follow one leader? Or is he simply saying that he needed something to break up the meeting, thought of the (old) saying, recognized its potential impact, and used it with no concern about whether it was applicable? Or, was he saying that he used it, believed it at the time, but now thinks the saying is wrong and divisive? In order to answer these questions, we have to know a great deal more: how he has used it before and how others have used it.

Nhlanhla Maake also commented on my use of the speech and pointed out there are many layers to this speech, and Mandela has artfully manipulated them to convey meaning. For instance, I can see how he goes from personal narrative to adage to manipulation of adage to application of story to the present, and then to a prescription for the audience in the form of "homework." But how pale my rendering is, and how exhilarating it was to experience a masterful storyteller who speaks to the very issues that are foremost on our minds.

I chose to start this book with President Mandela's speech not because I am an expert on Africa. That is not the case. I would be on safer ground talking about the Arctic and subarctic. I start with the speech because it illustrates to me, and I hope to you, how profound an impact story can have on us, even when our understanding is minimal. I chose an area that I did not know well to illustrate how important it is to know and have experiences with the particular group of people who tell the stories. As my African colleagues point out, there are depths of understanding in this story that I have not begun to know.

In this work, I want to suggest we think about the young children of the people gathered at that graduation. In some respects, they are like me. They will grow up in a world that will be different from their parents. How can we preserve a record that they will understand? What can we preserve of this experience? Tape recorders and video cameras can help, but they won't preserve meaning. What do future generations need to know to understand the record? That's what this work is all about.

The predicament we face with oral history is that recordings produce a fixed record of words that were spoken by one or more people to others at a particular time and place. Unfortunately, this record often tells us little or nothing about the original context of the story-telling, performance of the speakers, and reception/response of the audience.

Once recorded, we tend to treat stories as fixed commodities, as if they were containerized or freeze-dried. We forget that they were told at a particular time and place to particular people, and each telling represents a creative tension between a speaker who selectively recalls the past in order to speak to the present. The oral record that we have on tape represents one such telling. The tape may be played and replayed for many years. It may reside in a public archive along with many others. How can we be sure that future users have the best opportunities to move beyond the words on the tape to understand the meaning of what was shared?

Sometimes I hear people say how pleased they are that we have an extensive collection of recordings in our archive at the University of Alaska Fairbanks and that they preserve history and culture. As I realize more about the differences between stories told and stories recorded, I question just how good a job we are doing to preserve history and culture. I cringe a bit and ask myself what is missing from the archival record that was present in the recording session. Then I ask how does that session differ from what might occur when an elder decides to tell a story to a son or granddaughter? This book explores these questions, first through stories that naturally occur beyond reach of the recorder. We look at how people use story to convey meaning to each other and the implications for those of us who document, interpret, represent, and preserve these accounts. Then, we propose a new direction for curators of the oral record, a direction that can give the old tapes new life. But for the new approach to work we will need to break down some old distinctions and create a greater degree of understanding across academic lines.

We often create artificial distinctions between those who collect, those who research and report on, and those who preserve the record. When these are not the same person, their interests become compartmentalized, and there are too few opportunities to transfer understanding from recording session to future listeners and viewers of the record. This study brings together the work of several disciplines and celebrates the growing folklore and anthropology literature that speaks to how understanding of oral narrative is based on performance, setting, and context (Bauman and Briggs 1990; Finnegan 1992; 100–111; Toelken 1996; 117–56). This work is also firmly grounded in the realities of the curator of collections, who must serve the multiple and diverse interests of narrators, donors, and users. The goal is to incorporate each of the perspectives, interests, and approaches so that we can find ways to preserve more of what is going on when people decide to share their stories on tape for future generations.

The book begins with a quote by Chief Peter John, the traditional chief of the Tanana Chiefs region in central Alaska. Peter John knows how difficult it is to understand what is meant when people tell stories, and his teachings have stretched many of us to see multiple layers of meaning (Krupa 1996, 1999; Schneider 1998b). It is fitting that his words should lead us into this discussion. The full quote is discussed more fully in chapter three, "What's in a Story."

The subtitle is meant to highlight that there are cultural considerations in documentation, representation, and preservation of oral sources. The cultural issues are in some cases cross-cultural, which is to say we recognize distinct groups of people whose traditions and lifeways are different. At an individual level, this influences how we understand what they say, how they see themselves as members of a particular group, and how they recognize and define others.

In other cases, and at other times and places, it is more appropriate to speak of transcultural and cross-cultural patterning. I take the term transcultural patterning from Carolyn Hamilton, who used it in her critique of my discussion of the Nelson Mandela speech. There she used the term to describe to me the movement in South Africa to forge a common culture (personal communication, 1998). This lens has several advantages. It permits a more fluid view of peoples' lives; reflects the sharing of traditions that has occurred between groups; and in South Africa, it avoids the painful legacy of apartheid. During apartheid, cultures were viewed as separate and distinct static entities that could be identified and labeled. The labels were then used to justify the government's policies of segregation and discrimination. In a more recent exchange on the term "transcultural," Carolyn emphasized the ways people move beyond historical labels of culture to new identities that they actively create and from which they derive meaning. Considered in this way, transcultural patterning reflects the active role of individuals as both inheritors of identity and conscious shapers of new identities.[3]

I hadn't thought much about transcultural patterning in Alaska until I attended a memorial service for a prominent Native leader and his wife and daughter. They died in the tragic crash of Alaska

Airlines Flight 261 in February, 2000. As I listened to the eulogies for the three, I was struck by the fact that each of them not only walked in many worlds but also built lives that creatively and graciously introduced others to their heritage and experiences. While I know they saw themselves as Athabascan Indians first, one senses that is a quality and a range of experiences they brought to their fuller lives as civic leader, homemaker, and young woman who, among other things, guided the development of the World Extreme Skiing competition. The eulogies paid tribute to their Native heritage but presented them in this fuller light, as Alaskans, an umbrella that encompasses many influences.

Transcultural is differentiated from cross-cultural, which refers to the participation of individuals in one or more cultures at *different* times. In a simplified way, transcultural refers to commonly shared culture, whereas cross-cultural emphasizes the segmenting of lives into different dimensions shared with different groups at different times. For instance, an Inupiaq whale hunter may choose to participate in a National Guard meeting in Anchorage and share the same transcultural patriotic values for his country as the other Guard members from around the state. That same man may operate in cross-cultural contexts, such as his work both as an executive in a corporation and captain of a whaling crew. In the setting where he serves as executive for the corporation, there are certain standards of operation that are expected, and these may be very different from the standards and expectations that operate when he is serving on the whaling crew. For the corporation, he is called upon to make the maximum profits for the stockholders. On the whaling crew, he is called upon to feed the community.

But it is never this simple and clear cut. We all know that such categorizations are more useful to observers and describers than to participants. We all find ourselves mixing and matching, lumping and splitting experiences in very complex and not easily definable ways. Both the cultural and the transcultural lenses are merely constructs in each of our minds; they are not reality, although we all know what it feels like to be in situations where such categories make sense. Then, there are times when we are just confused and find all categories useless. I caution myself to keep in mind that these labels are no more than temporary road signs to warn me that my understanding of what is said and meant will in some cases be influenced by traditions different from my own. If I recognize and am conscious of the possibility and probability of differences, then I can be alert to this as I document, represent, and preserve what is said.

The order of steps listed on the title page of this book (documentation, representation, preservation, and interpretation) reflects the sequence of acquiring information (documentation), retelling it in some form for others to understand (representation), and preserving the meaning in multiple forms (preservation). Greg Sarris argues (1993, 5) that all information is processed against a backdrop of understandings and experiences; therefore, interpretation is implicit to documentation and each of the other steps. Following this thesis, one of the defining points of this work is the call for curators and researchers to interpret the record and represent their interpretations to others.

Some will argue that interpretation should not be a part of the preservation process. In this work, we take issue with that position and argue that we have to know what we are preserving, what it means, and why it is important in order to preserve it. Aware that our personal background may differ from that of the people who shared their stories, we need, on one hand, to keep cultural patterning in mind and, on the other, to see story as part of our own lives, to be open to the messages in personal ways. These dual tasks are not easy; they sometimes pull us in different directions: objective weighing of evidence akin to science, the search for ethical truths akin to philosophy, and the experiential, emotive, and expressive exploration that is more akin to art. Then, there are many times in my own experience when I don't know what is meant and I just have to be patient, persistent, and gain more experience before I can make an interpretation.

I hadn't been in South Africa for very long, and I was trying to buy a car. My friends Zakes and Wendy were with me in Johannesburg, where we met a used car salesman. Wendy and Phegello "Zakes" Letshela are young Northern Sotho; Wendy is a nurse and Zakes, at the time, was a librarian at the university. He has just finished his doctorate in information science and is now at the National Library of South Africa. Wendy has been to college and at the time was taking classes toward a degree. Both had lived through university years of turmoil and suppression and had stories to tell about the apartheid period. They are in solid support of the protests that helped bring about change. I still don't have a good idea of the used car salesman's background. He was White, middle-aged, and had apparently spent most of his life in South Africa. I do know from what he said that he was trying to come to grips with the changes that the downfall of apartheid had brought. We hadn't been in his car for more than three minutes when he asked me what I was going to do at the University of the North. I told him the library was interested in the history of current political leaders who got their education at this university. Zakes listed some of the prominent people. Then the salesman said, "But many of them spent time in jail." The three of us were confused as to what he meant. Did he mean that these leaders were somehow disgraced by serving time in jail as political criminals? Did he mean that they should not have crossed the line of disobedience no matter how right they were in their cause? Or was he just commenting on what to him was the irony of the transfer of power? What would it take to know what he really meant? If we heard him talk with his friends and in different settings then we might have a better idea what he meant.

In time I began to see that the University of the North's reputation as a center for resistance to the old apartheid government was, for some, a source of pride; for others it was ironic, and for some it was reprehensible. For instance, when I asked one of my colleagues at the University of the North, an Afrikaner professor, about some of the best students he had taught, he also noted that many of them were in positions of power, but he added, in a disapproving way, that they had spent time in jail. I realize now that breaking the law in the course of bringing about change for the better is a recurring issue for South Africans, particularly many Whites, who had all the advantages of a system of justice that favored them over the Blacks, Colored, and Indians. It is harder for them to recognize that change had to come, even though there was a cost to their way of life.

I still don't know what the used car salesman or the university professor really meant. In the present political climate, such feelings are masked, and I know the salesman and the professor far less well than Zakes and Wendy. Nevertheless, my experience gives me a better understanding of part of what they meant. Breaking the law in the name of any cause was something they had trouble understanding and supporting. The story also indicates that the gulf between their experiences and those of well-educated Blacks like Wendy and Zakes is immense.

Finding out what people mean takes time, an open mind, and exposure to lots of settings that give a framework for understanding the particular interchange. The words are not enough; we need to interpret, be open to revision, and build new understandings over time. A basic tenet of this work is that the struggle to understand what we record is as important as the struggle to physically preserve it.

Again, we return to the basic dilemma. Story is told in context, and each retelling is by definition a new context that, to use Verne Harris's term, "engages" others. And the more a story gets retold, the more it comes to be understood in a larger context. So in one way, we preserve in retelling—that is, we keep the story alive in people's minds and understandings, even though we remove the account from the original teller and context.

There is a two-way pull: should we interpret the meaning of the original telling and see story as a definable commodity or see story as speaking to a wide range of issues and concerns engaging people in new contexts with new meanings? The former approach attempts to put bounds and labels on story, and the latter attempts to see story as "fluid" (Hamilton 1997; Hofmeyer 1993).

The curator's dilemma is that he/she must understand both how the story has been and is used. In this work, I will argue that the recording is an artifact of a moment but its meaning is not bounded by the moment, and that the recording can only really make sense when considered against past and future tellings of the story. The tape recording is only a small piece of a much more complicated puzzle, with parts that are always changing shape. We preserve what we understand, and we understand by listening to how others engage the story, by reviewing other recordings, and by being very conscious of how our understandings are shaped. Ultimately, our understanding of story depends upon our ability to relate and identify with what is said, but it helps if we can trace in our own minds the basis of our understanding. That's not easy in cross-cultural and transcultural settings where we are never sure we got it, or will get it, right or, for that matter, what the range of "right" is at that moment.

This work is forged from about thirty years of experience listening and learning from Alaska Natives. I have had the personal pleasure to know and to work with some great teachers. I mention a few to introduce you to those who have influenced me most. My debt to them will be obvious as I draw upon their stories. Turak Newman was my first teacher, an Inupiaq man of extraordinary memory and storytelling ability (Newman n.d.). Moses Cruikshank, Turak's son-in-law, is an Athabascan man who first taught me the moral power of stories (Cruikshank 1986). Waldo Bodfish Sr. is an Inupiaq man whose life story chronicles the period of commercial whalers, reindeer herding, and the advent of airplane service to the North Slope of Alaska (Bodfish 1991). Howard Luke is an Athabascan man who lives in a log cabin in the shadow of Fairbanks and continually employs traditional teachings to impress on decision makers, teachers, students, and the interested public the need to respect the land and people (Jackson 1998). Chief Peter John is an extra special teacher, a man of great wisdom whose stories of love, *Ch'eghwetsen'*, have helped me in a very personal way to shape a more meaningful life (Schneider 1998b).

This work also grows out of my recent experiences in South Africa, where I had the chance to learn from African students and colleagues. The first draft of these essays was written during that stay (1997) with the intent of giving honors history students handouts that would help them to understand oral history. I consciously tried to use as many African examples as possible for their sake and to expand and test my own understanding. I had a lot of fun learning through these stories.

I am indebted to my friend and colleague Verne Harris formerly of the National Archives of South Africa and now Director of the South African History Archives. He has been a shaping influence in several ways. He introduced me to his own work (Harris 1996, 1997a, 1997b) and the work of other Africanists (Hamilton 1997; Hofmeyr 1993), scholars who helped me to better understand the potentials to reinvigorate the archival record with expanded meaning. Verne taught me to think of the archives as an institution for the future and to consider its documents as voices for and about the future, as well as the past. He and his friend and colleague from Canada, Terry Cook (Cook 1997), opened my eyes to the perspective of curator as both caretaker and responsible creator of records and, by extension, shaper of how we understand the human record.

The comparison of Alaska and South Africa has been personally very satisfying, although I must emphasize again that I am a student of Africa, not an expert. South Africa offers stimulating storytellers, colleagues that stretch my understanding, and a history of scholarship that helps me better understand in universal and in specific ways how people use stories to convey meaning.

I left for Africa in the winter of 1997 with the hope that the experiences would help me to gain a fuller understanding of Alaska and the role of storytelling. I returned to Alaska a short eleven months later with a comparative base, with examples from other settings where story plays a prominent part in the way people communicate meaning. I feel enriched. I also feel better equipped to address the disparity between the oral record sitting on the shelves of the library and the oral traditions and personal narratives that people choose to share with each other.

There are some interesting contrasts between Alaska and South Africa. In Alaska the oral record in the university archives goes back to the 1960s, with increased attention after 1980. In South Africa, researchers have been working for many years, and there is a depth of scholarship relating to oral narrative that should be of great interest to those of us who work in the United States. On the other hand, South African efforts to build a broad and public record of oral sources are fairly recent. There are some notable collections, but the effort at a national level is still in the beginning stages. So, there are wonderful opportunities to shape how the programs are set up and to benefit from African scholarship. The recent seminar series at the University of Witwatersrand, "Reinventing the Archives" (Oct. 1998) was a promising launch that brought together a combination of scholarship in narrative analysis and archival theory.

We might think of public oral history collection in South Africa as a great ship preparing to embark from the harbor, gaining speed and setting course, whereas we might think of public oral history collections in Alaska as an equally great ship far along on a voyage under full power, but realizing that there is a need to change course and slowly beginning to make that change. The former is setting course, the latter is changing course. Both cases face the preservation challenge, which is to recognize the personal, situational, cultural, and historical factors that influence storytelling, to document the way narrative is constructed and performed, and to continually bring new understandings to the representation and preservation of the record. To do this we must recognize that we are preserving understandings within context and setting. These understandings take on meaning as they are viewed against the backdrop of other tellings and other times (Hatang 2000, 27). Preservation of meaning, like physical preservation, is an ongoing task and we must focus on both. This represents a fundamental shift in how we should train and prepare curators of the oral record. While the dynamics described in this book are most obvious in cross-cultural settings, they are also critical to any understanding of an oral record.

I have written these essays using lots of stories because that is the way we must think if we are to understand how people communicate. I also hope they are fun to read and that they help make the discussion realistic and meaningful. The book is somewhat of a personal journey with stories, a way to illustrate how understanding is an ongoing endeavor, enlivened by new insights gained from the old tellings and the new opportunities for retellings.

We begin with a rather personal chapter about my experiences with the people who helped me learn how to listen to stories, a bit of context on how I have been shaped by people who are masterful with story. The second chapter is a wide-ranging discussion of story and the many forms it can take, kind of a stretching exercise, although by no means totally inclusive. Then I discuss how oral tradition and oral history differ and how the distinction can be our most important guide as we try to decipher and use the oral record. Chapters four, five, six, and seven explore four types of story genre. First, there are the personal narratives, building blocks for oral tradition. Personal narratives are like the meat in a stew; they are discernable chunks that add flavor and texture throughout the dish—in this case, throughout the book. Personal narratives are briefly introduced in chapter three, "What's in a Story". Then, they are discussed in chapter four, "Sorting out Oral Tradition and Oral History." Because of their broad significance, they are the specific subject of chapter five, are the subject of analysis in chapter seven, and are further discussed in chapter eight as the basis of life histories. Most of what we call oral history consists of personal accounts of what someone has experienced or witnessed, information that may never become part of a group's collective knowledge and is best described as personal narrative.

Chapter six is about formal gatherings organized to bring people together to tell stories or to speak about particular topics, such as land claims or traditional leadership. I affectionately refer to this as the forgotten genre because it produces a large record that is rarely consulted after the event. Chapter seven discusses directed interviews, where interviewers and narrators work together to expand understanding of topics. Often the interviewer produces a product based on the interviews. Next comes life histories based on oral narrative, what I call the constructed genre because it often involves collaboration of the interviewee and the interviewer to produce a joint product, the story of the interviewee's life. The last three chapters build on a rising tide of concerns raised in the other chapters about use of story and the differences between a private and public record. Ethical concerns about how stories are used, managed, and retold permeate this manuscript and are as vital a fluid to its health as water is to our bodies. We choose to tell stories, one to another; they become part of our social fabric, ways to share with each other, but they are given and received with hope and concern about how they will be interpreted and retold. Often we only partially and crudely understand what we are told, so we are continually reevaluating what we know, how we know what we know, and what we think is appropriate to talk and write about with others. Many of our most important clues come from the oral tradition, how others choose to remember, retell, and pass on story one to another. There is always an ethical responsibility to consider these questions in our work with narrative.

The concluding chapter presents the preservation challenge: what can we do to preserve a fuller and more meaningful public oral record?

I have used a variety of ways to refer to people: full names, first names, last names, full title, and nicknames. I hope this will convey a sense of how I know the individuals, how we relate to each other, and indirectly, how I have learned from them. When I reference tape recordings, these refer to either the collections at the Elmer Rasmuson Library or the Alaska Native Language Center Collection.

Turak Newman and Ida Edwards in Beaver in
front of Ida's house. Photo by Bob Betts.

Moses Cruikshank in the Oral History Office, University of Alaska Fairbanks.
Photo by David Nelson.

right: Waldo Bodfish outside his house in Wainwright. In his last years, he couldn't go far, but he always found ways to connect with the natural world. Eventually, his front steps became his vantage point for observations.

below: Howard Luke making a dog sled at the Howard Luke Academy. He is a patient teacher, and it has been my privilege to know and learn from him. Photo by Bill Burke.

A Career Full of Stories

Fresh from graduate school at Bryn Mawr College in the suburbs of Philadelphia, I arrived in Alaska. I had received a well-rounded education in anthropology, and I was fortunate to study with some of the best teachers I've ever met. But all of that was far removed from the realities of life in rural northern communities. Fortunately I knew that the years I spent on the "main line" were a rarified life, and I tried to prepare myself for a life that could balance university and community.

The Village of Beaver

My first trip to Alaska was in 1972, and that is when I first went to Beaver and met some of the people who have played so prominently in my understandings of story, Turak Newman and Moses Cruikshank. Back then the trip to Fairbanks was an easy nonstop Pan American flight, six hours from New York. The mail plane schedule from Fairbanks to Beaver was nowhere near as accommodating—three days a week, weather permitting. That was still easier than the lengthy steamboat trip that was the customary route when my advisor worked in the interior of Alaska.[4]

After a few days in Fairbanks I was off to Beaver. Elman Pitka was the chief and the mail carrier. I remember he met the plane with a wheelbarrow, and as he wheeled the mail into the village post office, I asked him where I might set up my tent and if it was all right for me to do research. He connected me with Turak Newman, and we began a collaboration that has enriched my life immensely. I was an eager student, and he was an excellent teacher with a precise memory, a sense of history, and an engaging way to present it.

I explained to people that I wanted to study Indians and Eskimos, to figure out how they learned to live together. There are many stories about how these groups don't get along, stories about bloody battles and revenge killings. Recent scholarship reveals that there are

also stories about acts of kindness between members of each group
and in some places, like the Koyukuk River and Beaver, the record
also shows a recent history of intermarriage (Clark 1974, 180–85;
Arundale and Jones 1989, 151). What is unusual about Beaver is that
it is located on the Yukon River, deep in Athabascan territory. How
and why did Eskimos end up there? My advisor Frederica de Laguna
had a colleague, Annette Clark, who was at the National Museum of
Man in Ottawa and had done work with people living on the Koyukuk
River in communities of Indians and Eskimos. She knew about and
was interested in Beaver because it had some Koyukon speakers who
had come upriver from Stevens Village. She suggested it would be a
good place to work.

I remember distinctly that hot summer afternoon in Beaver. I was
sitting in Grandma Charlotte Adams's house. Her daughter turned to
me and said, "We do not want to be put under a microscope."
Somehow, I had to figure out what to do. And, as I was to learn many
times over, this initial point of discussion is critical. Without the coop-
eration, interest, and collaboration of the people, there is no chance
to understand what they know and no right to use their information.
I was to learn that this process of negotiation and collaboration over
research approach doesn't end after the interviews are done; it continues right on through the preservation of tape in an archive, for as
long as peoples' stories are under consideration.

As I listened to Turak tell stories about the trail north to the gold
mining areas, I figured out an approach. I could study the history of
the community and in so doing come to understand my research question—how Indians and Eskimos live peacefully together in this place.
History was acceptable and of interest to the community because they
recognized the value of their ancestors' experiences, and they knew
that very little had been written about that. Back at Bryn Mawr that
fall, I began to formulate a proposal that eventually would fund a
return trip for a year's study. The idea was to compile life stories and
to then look at common trends and compare experiences.

I didn't get back to Beaver until late the following fall, as the ice
was running in the Yukon River. Again I stayed with Turak and right
away we were hard at work. He provided the scaffolding and many of
the details on the movement of Eskimo people into Beaver. His stories
were always told with great attention to detail and with dialogue that
transported me back in time to the action. Years after I heard the stories, I realized that he was also very skillful at preparing the listener

with just enough context about who is speaking and then breaking into dialogue without direct reference to "he said" or "she said." Instead, the context and the terms of reference in the dialogue make it clear who is speaking, a bit like a play.

I remember his account:

> When Bob hired me, he said, "you come up in June." I said, "yes." So I started packing in the middle part of June. I was pretty strong in those days. I started out with seventy-five pounds on my back. I traveled at night because it was cooler. Well, I went as far as five miles out. The mosquitoes were terribly bad. I came back that same night and slept all day. I told mother, Old Molly, "I'm going to try it again tomorrow." Mother, first place did not want me to go. "Son, you never been on that trail. You have two streams to cross. You don't know how to build a raft." I said, "Mother, don't worry about that; I have helped people make a raft." "Yes, but something might happen to you." (Newman n.d., 16–17)

Unlike Turak, there were some people who didn't want to share their stories for the "official record"; I didn't fully realize then that there are differences between what people may choose to share amongst themselves and what they may want an outsider like myself to record and represent to the world. One afternoon, I was sitting with Moses Cruikshank and his sister's son Artie. Moses was telling one of his great stories about gold mining or mushing dogs in the Interior. When he was done, I began to ask questions and Artie cut me off right away. It was his way of saying, this story you heard was a gift; don't be impolite and ask for more. And further, the story was told for us at this time; it wasn't meant to be taken down and used by you for your own ends. Years later, when the time was right, I was asked to record Moses's story. And, fortunately, he was also ready to present his life to a wider audience (Cruikshank 1986).

I'm still trying to learn how to make public oral recordings in ways that respect all of the interested parties. As a curator of collections, I now realize that the interested parties include the narrator who shared the story, the narrator's community members, the researcher who did the recording, the archive that must manage the record, and future researchers who may want to use it in their work. When I am the curator of the materials, I sit in the middle and try to reach a plan that is sensitive to each of the interested groups and can

be reasonably followed. But back then I didn't have all of the interest groups clearly in mind, and I was just beginning to think about
people who might want to use the tapes in the future.

My work in Beaver was based on a series of life stories that I recon-
structed from the personal narratives. When I compared these stories,
I was able to draw some conclusions about the common experiences of
each ethnic group. But common experiences don't necessarily mean
that everyone tells the same story. I learned in Beaver that different
people would probably emphasize different aspects of a particular
experience in their stories. This is the strength of the oral record—you
get more than one side of the story. For instance, in telling about the
two major migrations of people to Beaver from the Arctic Coast, Turak
only briefly mentioned that Ida Edwards had a baby along the way.
Instead, he emphasized the people they met and the route they followed. Ida's story was all about how the minister-doctor was worried
about her going, about relatives she felt she might be leaving behind,
and about what it was like to give birth on the trail:

> "Well," I told the doctor, "I make up my mind, I'm going." I did
> go, too. He didn't want me to go. I tried to talk to Newman to stay
> here till I have my baby. He said that he had to come home. Finally,
> I made up my mind. I go! Here I am left all alone. Well, my father
> got no wife, my grandmother there. My grandmother was old, too.
> Just before I decided to go, she got sick, heart failure or something
> [and she died]. That is why I go.
>
> I don't remember where he took us, around the coast. I don't
> know where we swing down this way. There were reindeer herders
> there; Alfred Hopson was there. From there, I don't know which way
> they took us.
>
> We went inland, toward Allashuk's family. Olla and his wife also
> camp there. That is where the baby was born, Iktalikpok (Itqiliqpaat).[5]
> Maggy, Howard, a few of them [children were there] anyway. We came
> to that place, Iktalikpok, tiny house there. All of us there—Allashuk,
> his wife and kids, Olla and his wife, Bob, Newman, and Blanche and
> me and Ed.
>
> Oh gosh, right there I got sick. Ed found out, "Are you getting
> sick?" I said, "Yes, I think so." Well, no room, where I going to have
> it? . . . so they made up a canvas tent for me outside and they heated
> it up out there. They picked me up [and carried me in there]. They
> thought that I had it, no doctors. [They thought she would die.]

No trouble. That old man Allashuk, he is religion. He pray for me right there, no trouble. Blanche was there with me. Two days we stayed there till I got stronger. (Schneider 1976, 434–435)

After completing fieldwork, I returned to the East Coast to write the dissertation. Dr. de Laguna knew that I didn't have much money and that I had this Alaskan dog with me. Bryn Mawr had just purchased a Catholic girls' school, and she negotiated for me and my dog Smoky to be the caretakers. It was a very nice setup, but I longed to get back to Alaska.

An opportunity developed with the National Park Service, and I jumped on it. I was hired to document and describe the significance of Native historic sites. As part of the Alaska Native Claims Settlement Act, the Native regional corporations had the opportunity to select historic and cemetery sites to own and manage. The Park Service, as the lead federal agency for historic preservation, helped the corporations in the documentation stage. Field testing came later and was done by the Bureau of Indian Affairs and the Bureau of Land Management. In many respects, my job was great. I got to travel to many more communities, and I met some wonderful storytellers. I remember one night with Johnny Frank in Venetie—the old man went on and on into the night. I wish now that I had listened more closely and recorded his stories on tape. I cherish the memory of that old man running down the trail, pipe in mouth, with a broad welcoming smile on his face.[6] We received the same warm welcome from David Salmon in Chalkyitsik and Maggie Gilbert in Arctic Village.

Back then, the challenge was to present Native concepts of sites to an audience of non-Natives, people used to buildings or archaeological sites with lots of tangible remains and associations with what we have come to recognize as major events and prominent personalities—mansions and old buildings where unusual and outstanding events took place. In contrast, many of the sites people were telling us about had few remains; they were subsistence use areas, places that were good for hunting, trapping, and fishing, but no less historical. They represented the historical patterning of activities from an earlier era. I was forced to think about how these individual sites fit into a yearly cycle of use and how that reflected an adaptation to a way of life at a particular point in time. In other cases, the sites represented ancient history. For instance, I remember a story Susan Hansen recorded about the giant shrew that lived on Nunivak Island. There were geographic features that told of his activities, the place where he lay down, where his tail rested, and the islands he used as stepping stones when hunting for whales and seals (Hansen n.d.; Bureau of Indian Affairs 1995; Drozda and Amos 1997).

The challenge was to mate Western concepts of historic preservation as embodied in the 1966 National Historic Preservation Act with the realities of the rural Alaskan environment and very different cultural traditions. One of the first tests of how well this would work came with some sites on the North Slope.

On the North Slope

My boss in the Park Service was Zorro Bradley. Zorro was a career Park Service man, but he certainly didn't fit the mold. Zorro was head of the Cooperative Park Studies Unit, where he had responsibilities for the Native historic and cemetery site program and documenting subsistence. An archaeologist by training, he also recognized the importance of story. The thing about Zorro that stands out most in my mind is how he could see opportunities, get money to do projects, and have enough confidence in the people who worked for him to let them go and do good work.

That's what happened on the North Slope. Zorro got wind of the plans for a big study of resource values in the National Petroleum Reserve in Alaska, a huge stretch of the North Slope stretching from the Utukok River in the west to the Colville River in the east and inland to the Brooks Range. I was assigned to work with the North Slope Borough to begin a program to document sites in the reserve and to get them established on the National Register of Historic Places, the principal way to ensure a level of consideration in the course of development on federal land. I think Zorro figured that if we were doing work on the Slope there would be a place for us on the big interagency team that was sure to be formed. He was right. The first work I did was in Wainwright, some eighty miles west of Barrow. There again, I had the good fortune to team up with an exceptional local historian, Waldo Bodfish Sr. (Kusiq).

Waldo and other elders prioritized the important places to research on the Kuk River. Their oral accounts and our site visits were the basis for National Register nominations for several places on the river. To the casual visitor these places were not exceptional—house pits, caribou bones, plywood shipping crates used as siding on small shelters—hardly Mount Vernon. Yet taken as a whole and viewed within the context of a pattern of use, these places represent an important part of the history of the people who now reside in Wainwright. The remains represent only a small part of the significance. The real story was in the reconstruction of a way of life, and that could only be told by the people who had lived it. Their stories made the sites come alive with meaning. It's not the type of thing that one learns after one visit. I was fortunate to be able to revisit some of the places and to spend lots of time with elders who had lived there (Ivie and Schneider 1978, 1988; Bodfish 1991).

A visit to the sites with elders is, in some respects, like looking at pictures—the old places stimulate recall of stories and prompt questions from the newcomer. But here, as in so much oral information, the individual story has to be placed within a context of other sites and other tellings. This points to a fundamental lesson that all students of oral history must learn from oral tradition. To really understand what a story means, we must hear it many times and place it within the context of other stories and other types of information such as the written and archaeological records. Our understanding of the particular depends, in part, on our general knowledge. In the oral tradition, one can expect to hear many stories over a period of time, and in the normal course of daily activities we experience enough to reconstruct the commonly known local historical knowledge.

As obvious as all this is, I still make the mistake of thinking that I can make a recording or listen to a recording and have sufficient background to understand and assess the information that is shared. I must remind myself to take my cue from oral tradition, be patient, and reflect the particular against the backdrop of many tellings.

Unlike in Beaver, almost everyone on the North Slope speaks their Native language, Inupiaq. My work probably suffered because I didn't learn the language, but I had the pleasure of doing most of my work with Waldo. He spoke excellent English, and he told lots of his stories in English, even though his first language was Inupiaq. I began a life history with Waldo in English, but I found that I still needed help from Native speakers who knew both their language and their culture well, people who could help translate linguistic concepts from English and Inupiaq. Out of this work came a wonderful collaboration with two experts: Leona Okakok and James Nageak. Without their help, I couldn't do justice to the richness of Kusiq's stories.

I remember one time we were working on his story about the first animal that he killed and how his parents asked him to give it to an old woman in the village. This established an important relationship between the young hunter and the old woman. Waldo continued to give her food and she helped him. When Leona read Waldo's English account, she explained: "One of the most important gifts the elder provides is to appeal for the hunter's success. The Inupiaq term is 'Ququq,' as in 'Ququgniaqtun,' which means, 'I will call upon everything I can for (your) success'" (Bodfish 1991, 267).

Without Leona's help, my full understanding of the relationship would not include the old woman's call for spiritual help to aid young Waldo.[7] As so often would be the case, I was learning that when we record, translate, and transcribe concepts cross-culturally, we must translate meaning, not just words, and this means interpretation. And interpretation is based on experience, a point illustrated in another story from that work.

Waldo was telling James and me a whale-hunting story in Inupiaq. When James translated the story for me the first time, he produced a literal word-for-word translation. I remember thinking that, in no time, perhaps over lunch, we could smooth out the rough edges and make the story understandable for a Western audience. Well, it wasn't that simple. As James went through the story, there were lots of details about whale hunting that were part of specialized hunter's knowledge. Even with a translation, I didn't have the background to understand the subject the way it was presented.

James ended up producing both a literal and an interpretative translation. That way, an Inupiaq whaler could read the literal and also compare it with the interpretative translation. I was learning that with specialized knowledge, the translation to a second language is dependent on the experiences as well as the linguistic skills of the translator. If the subject is something that is in the domain of women's knowledge, then a male translator may not be qualified to translate.

The example I gave was of a translation, but this is also true of stories retold in the same language. Translation, like retelling of any story, depends to some extent on interpretation by both the reteller and the audience. As I noted in the introduction, Greg Sarris, in his work *Keeping Slug Woman Alive,* follows David Murray (1991) in reminding us so clearly that "description cannot be separated and made prior to interpretation" (1993, 5). Interpretation is based on experience, and there must be some level of common experience for a story to have meaning to an audience. Without common understanding of the topic, it is impossible to imagine what is said. That's why I believe so strongly that curators of collections must know the subjects discussed if they are going to adequately preserve the recordings, and this necessarily involves a level of interpretation.

The Peaceful Revolution

In 1980, I joined the University of Alaska Fairbanks and established the Oral History Program in the Alaska and Polar Regions Department. Six years later, the university went through a severe budget crisis and my program was cut deeply. I had to do something to ensure preservation and access to the recordings whether there was curatorial help or not. During those dark days we weren't thinking much about preservation of understanding; we were focused on survival, an approach that would keep the tapes safe, in order, and accessible to researchers despite lowered staff levels in the office.

That is what was in the back of my mind over Thanksgiving vacation when I headed out on a camping trip with my friend Felix Vogt, a Swiss graduate student in business management. He suggested the possibility of electronic technology to preserve and retrieve recordings. At that early stage, the idea was to digitize recordings and to retrieve them from the computer. Felix ended up writing a master's paper on the subject and getting a grant from the Apple Library of Tomorrow to develop a prototype program. Since that start, we have added photos, maps, and texts to interactive computer-based programs based on interviews with people from different regions of the state.

We call these programs "jukeboxes" because the user selects recordings to hear and then the computer pulls them up with associated text, maps, and photos. We now have thirty or so programs from all over the state of Alaska, and some of the jukeboxes are delivering fifty to sixty hours of audio and lots of other information, some of it organized according to key words. In all there are about four hundred hours of audio in digital form.

Headaches from Technology

The technology gives us headaches when it refuses to work, but it has opened up new possibilities and allowed us to change the way we do oral history. Ironically, what began as a desperate move to automate in a budget-cutting period has become a better way to preserve meaning. Now, we can include with each recording information on the context of the interviews, the circumstances under which the tape was made, and background information helpful to the audience. It is all together so that you can listen to a recording, view a picture, or go to a map and click on a place to hear about its history.

In each case, we will be able to return to communities a program that features their original recordings. From an historical perspective, the beauty of this approach is that it allows us to give the user multiple perspectives on the topics. For this reason, it has been very popular in rural communities. The people don't feel that their words have been taken out of context or misinterpreted or that there is a search for one "correct" interpretation. Of course, interpretation in the contextualizing, screen design, choice of images, texts, maps, and even in the way key words are chosen is a critical part of what we are doing, but this is qualitatively different from the traditional report or manuscript format where narrators are talked about and the author is viewed as the expert voice.

In the jukebox, users choose speakers to hear as opposed to being led by an expert's analysis. In Alaska, Native groups are tired of outsiders interpreting them. They argue that outsiders always get it wrong and don't know enough about the culture to understand what they have said. The jukeboxes will, I think, address this concern and give future researchers a broad base to compare different accounts. They can then draw on and reference these narrators in their work. The communities will have the original speaker's presentations for reference in cases where they think elders were misquoted. The potential to create historical dialogue between academics and community members based on the programs is immense.

The challenge has been to construct these technologically complicated programs, to keep them operational at remote sites, and to find ways to integrate them into the curriculum. We know we are headed in the right direction programmatically, but the technical challenges and the ethical issues raised by network and other forms of distribution are daunting. We are about to provide network access to our programs, and despite considerable discussion, we are quite nervous about how narrators will feel about worldwide access to their stories.

The Archives

Unfortunately, my dream that this technology would allow us to digitize the entire oral history collection of over eight thousand recordings has not happened. Instead, we have lots of new recordings from projects funded to produce jukeboxes. I have not abandoned the dream: when we can, we digitize the old recordings and try to give them new life.

It seems there is never enough time or money to fully meet the needs for preservation and access, and we are continually weighing what is most important to do next. The new challenge is to link the jukebox programs so that users at remote sites will be able to access all of them at once. Imagine sitting in a place like Dillingham and being able to access on-line over four hundred hours of audio. As exciting as this possibility is, the challenge has raised ethical issues. Even though narrators signed release forms making the information available through the archives, did they ever imagine that it would be available to the world at the click of a mouse?

We are still trying to resolve how public people want their information to be and to understand a range of concerns about interpretation and representation. In many communities there is concern about outsiders misinterpreting information and exploiting the information for their own ends. All of this is part of a bigger question about the rights of researchers and the rights of the people they research. On one hand, there is a long tradition of academic freedom, but there is also an awakening sensitivity to the rights of people to have a say in how their information and performances are represented and presented in public forums. This is an issue that will not easily be resolved because it strikes at the heart of some very basic differences in philosophy. In the Western tradition, individual choice and decision-making is highly valued. If a person decides to tell a story and release it to an archive, it is considered their business and their right, even though others in the community may disagree with what was said. In Native cultures, there are other entities such as the clan (in Southeast Alaska) and the community who also have interests that are not represented under Western law.

Of course, the more complex question is how to inform future users that the recordings are sensitive and that community permission should be sought for projects in which someone wants to usurp an entire story or recording. Like the questions of meaning discussed earlier, ethical issues are best understood against a broad backdrop of experience. Sometimes we just have to admit that we don't know how to respond and that the best thing to do is to wait and keep talking with all of the interested parties.

None of the big questions were resolved by the spring of 1997 when I left for South Africa. In fact, they still aren't resolved now in

2002, although I think we are more aware of the issues and better able to inform contributors and researchers.[8]

Off to South Africa

My colleague Rich Seifert alerted me to an announcement of a Fulbright opportunity for someone to go to the Northern Province in South Africa and help the University of the North establish an oral history program. Early in January, with temperatures around -50 F, I left my wife, daughter, and the furnace repair man and boarded a plane that would take me on the first leg of my trip to South Africa. I arrived at the tail end of the African summer and settled in to help the library staff establish a program to document the history of the university (Schneider, Mathibhe, and Maqoko 1997) As noted in the introduction, this was quite a contrast to my Alaska responsibilities. In South Africa, I was helping to start, as opposed to inheriting, a collection. We had the chance to do everything right, and it was a chance for me to think long and hard about what I had learned in the years at Rasmuson Library. One of the interesting things was that many of the ethical issues that I left in Alaska had not surfaced in South Africa. I found myself continually raising these questions for consideration.

We took our time, met once a week, carefully planned our approach, did background research, and avoided the oral history nemesis: we did a few interviews well, as opposed to trying to capture the experiences of everyone all at once.

When I left for South Africa, I hoped for experiences that would give me different ways to understand storytelling in Alaska and, more generally, how people use story to create and convey meaning. In South Africa, I was surrounded by stories. Africans seem to dance and sing their stories and they mark occasions with praise poems.

Even before the plane had made its way to the end of the runway at Kennedy International Airport, I was tuned to the in-flight programming of African stories. In the months ahead, I would see and hear the use of traditional sayings to express meaning on television, over luncheon conversations, and in governmental directives. Each of these expressions and sayings is a reminder of something to value and direct us in life.

The importance of story was also recognized by the Information Studies Department at the university. They asked me to teach about oral history in the beginning and advanced library classes, and one of their faculty was engaged in researching what she terms the "oral information system." By this she means the ways community members orally pass on information to each other and how this might be incorporated in the efforts of librarians and other information specialists. All of this was quite different from my experiences at Rasmuson Library in Fairbanks, where I had never been asked to contribute to the library teaching and where stories in the oral history collection have been viewed more as a source for specific pieces of information rather than as a way of thinking about and coming to know the world.

This last point has direct bearing on how I began to envision the role and challenges of preserving public oral history collections. Suffice it to say here that my experiences in South Africa added momentum to a growing conviction that I had to find ways to preserve more than words on a tape, that the issue was meaning. To understand meaning I had to be open to learning how people think, experience, and act, as well as consider the literal transcript of what they say. I had to be a caretaker of knowledge, not just tapes. I had to understand the "oral information system." And I had to continually reevaluate against a backdrop of past, present, and future tellings.

Kathy Ahgeak and Walter Akpik documenting sites on the Meade River.

Horace Ahsogeak with David Libbey on the Lower Meade River documenting sites.

Bill Schneider with Frederica de Laguna on one of
her trips to Fairbanks. Colleagues, graduate students,
and advanced undergraduate students affectionately
refer to her as "Freddy." Photo by Holly Reckord.

University of the North campus in South Africa.

Dr. Phegello "Zakes" Letshela in front of the
National Library of South Africa where he is now
programme executive, collections management.

Left to right, Sello Hatang, deputy director of the South African History
Archives and coordinator of its Freedom of Information Program; Verne
Harris, director of the South African History Archives; and Ethel Kriger, for-
merly of the National Archives and now a history Ph.D. student at the
University of South Africa, where she will be researching the Truth and
Reconciliation Commission and issues of social memory.

# What's in a Story⁹

Stories from Generation to Generation

We strained to hear Howard Luke as airboats and motorboats raced up and down the Tanana River and jet planes roared overhead. Despite the urban noises and our proximity to Fairbanks just across the river, here the smell of wood smoke and the cool breezes off the river helped transport us back to a more reflective time. We were back in the 1930s, Howard's mother was alive, and there were others who made this a village of Athabascans. We listened as he told stories and related his traditional knowledge to modern issues such as the Army Corps of Engineers dredging of the Chena, plans for an electric intertie, and the need to respect and conserve resources such as water and game.

Howard told the old story of the young girl who broke the taboos of her puberty seclusion and turned from the wall to look out into the bright sunlight. On the hill she saw sheep, and, unable to help herself, she yelled the news to her mother. Immediately, the sheep turned to stone. Whenever we see the white stones on the hillside, these are the sheep that were transformed to stone when the girl failed to respect herself and the animals. How many times has this old story been told, how many times have the white stones been mentioned, and what sort of a reminder is this to each of us to take responsibility for our actions and show respect for the resources we depend upon? (See also Luke 2000, 106.)

Howard's story reminds me of the well-known account from Southeast Alaska about how the glacier advanced in Glacier Bay and wiped out the village, all because a young woman in seclusion made the fatal mistake of mocking the glacier (Jones in Dauenhauer and Dauenhauer 1987, 245–59). Are we in some ways like these young women, undisciplined in our relationship with the environment, unmindful of our responsibilities, and ripe to make mistakes with severe consequences to our survival?

Stories like these live in our minds and in our senses, a point that Keith Basso made when he described how the Apache landscape is made real and moral when Indians travel to places imbued with stories of past events. The stories and the places work together to remind us of how to live on this land (1996, 37–70). Stories are timeless, they can describe events that occurred in the distant past, before anyone can remember, yet they also carry a message that continues to be relevant to our lives today. In an indirect way they remind us of how our actions may be similar to those described in the story, and we are called upon to pay attention and apply the message to our lives.

In these cases, setting shapes experience. Howard's camp is a step back in time, yet it is right there in the jet path of a modern city, and he tells these stories not just to preserve history but to equip us with knowledge and a reality we should not ignore. The event (a class of teachers) and the place (Howard's camp) are the reason and the setting for his story and are linked to what he thinks we should know: we have to respect nature.

This is a common theme in Howard's stories, and he often warns not to "go against nature." By this he means doing things that adversely impact the environment and natural resources or even going against the way nature works. I was reminded of this last point most recently when he commented about bending birch for sled parts. We were gathered at the Howard Luke Academy and surrounded by students when he said that it was cheating to steam birch, that the way to shape sled runners was to choose good straight birch, then it will bend easily and not break, but if you choose crooked birch and steam it to bend, then it will not be strong and will break. In Howard's reasoning, steaming goes against nature and is cheating.

Stories like this one told to teach a lesson, are linked to the teller's recognition that the audience needs to know something important.

From the other side of the world, Joseph Sheppherd lived with Ntumu people in the rainforests of Cameroon and studied the way they used proverbs. One day, Papa Atanga was preparing honey on a leaf and he decided to share a proverb with Joseph. He said, "Man is a leaf of honey." He went on to say, "Man is good and man is precious and, like the leaf of honey, his goodness is inexhaustible. When you think that there is none left, there is still some there to find. This you should not forget" (Sheppherd 1988, 4–5). To understand this, Joseph needed to know that the honey that Papa Atanga had collected on the leaf would go to his first wife, who would drain it into a bottle. Then she would give the leaf to the children, who would lick it, and then they would throw it to the goats, who would lick it, and then to the ants, flies, and other insects.

Once Joseph knew how it was used, he was ready to hear and understand Papa Atanga's command that this was something he should not forget, that sharing and mutual dependence were basic precepts of their society. In this case, the setting where he saw the leaf used to transport honey was the tangible starting place for Atanga's story, and the sharing of the honey was the basis for Joseph to understand the proverb. As with Howard and his stories, we must build up background and pay close attention to the context in which the story is shared.

When I first got to South Africa, I stayed in a place that had a television, and one of the shows I tried never to miss was the Sunday night reports on the Truth and Reconciliation Commission hearings.[10] By far the most interesting and touching part of these reports was the coverage of people returning to the scenes of past atrocities to describe how and where things happened. In these cases, the setting is part of the retelling and, in some cases, part of the grieving process for those who have suffered the loss of loved ones.

Occasion also triggers story. For instance, an African praise poem may be the way to introduce an important person. The occasion and the presence of an important person and audience are ceremonially marked by the performance of a praise singer, a person skilled in oratory and knowledgeable to introduce and comment (see Finnegan 1970, 83–118). For instance, when Walter Sisulu, a famous freedom fighter during the apartheid years, was recognized for his efforts with the city of Johannesburg's highest honor, the Freedom of the City metal, a Xhosa praise singer was called to address the audience (Jacobson 1997, 3).

At a Communities of Memory storytelling session in Nome, Alaska, on the Bering Sea and truly as far geographically from South Africa as one can be, Job Kokochurak chose a timely occasion to tell about how to read the weather.[11] Hunters had been caught out in a storm and had suffered badly. Job said:

> Recently, before there were men frozen, you know what I was watching in Nome? Five days. There was signaling that the storm was coming. Five days. Every day I see the signal. The bad weather never come. Possibly those men that freezed to death see that and when it

never happened they went ahead and go out in the country. Then they're in the news and we learned what they'd been doing. I put that out for you just to save your life possibly. When it signal once that bad weather generally come in three days. But if it signal but never happens for a matter of time, it's real dangerous. So watch your sun and for the indication of a storm up in the sky. If it never happens, the more dangerous it is when it comes. This is the way the old people used to talk long ago. (Communities of Memory, Nome, February 15 and 16, 1996, in Sabo 1997, 32)

Performance of story can take many different forms. Years ago, Barre Toelken gave one of the most interesting and entertaining lectures I have ever attended, and in part of his presentation he played and sang traditional folk songs from different parts of the world. I was moved by his guitar playing and his singing, but he did something else. He provided commentary on the songs. Barre, like many other folklorists, realizes that songs are a rich source of stories that continue to speak to issues such as social justice, bravery, and patriotism.[12]

Songs and dances are stories performed with music and motion. Sometimes, like the praise poem, these story-songs will be composed for specific people and occasions. In Alaska, some Athabascan Indian people have memorial potlatch songs, which are their way to remember and commemorate a person who has passed away. Generally these are first sung publicly a year or so after the person's death at a special ceremony called a potlatch. This concludes the formal period of mourning. Peter John has shared many of these songs with me because they reflect the way Athabascans show love to each other, what he calls Ch'eghwetsen'. One of the memorial potlatch songs describes how a man has lost his brother, and when he thinks of him, he pictures a stick bobbing in the river current, pushed down by the water and the ice, but continuing to resurface. The memory keeps coming back. The words to part of the song are, "Who's going to replace my brother. I miss him pretty bad but I got to have a brother, through him only I'm going to live" (notes from 6/30/95). Peter says, "When Indians make song, they make sure that it will help other people." This example, like Howard's of bending sled runners, paints a vivid picture, in this case of resiliency and the importance of our love for siblings. That old stick bobbing in the current of a mighty river like the Tanana or the Yukon becomes a powerful symbol of resiliency and steadfastness.

While stories can be told in many different forms—songs, dances, tales, proverbs, and even jokes—Barre Toelken reminds us that each form has its own set of requirements: "We can assume, however, that certain features encourage dynamism. Any folksong or poem that depends for much of its effect on rhyme or rhythm will tend to change more slowly than such freer prose narratives as the joke or memorate. Within a tale or a song, certain striking phrases or recurrent, formulaic conventions are likely to be retained . . . while other features of the same text may be quite open to continual change" (1996, 41).

When Stories are Personal

So far, many of the stories I've mentioned are known and shared by a group of people. There are also stories that are known only by a few people and are recognized as a person's story. In South Africa, and in the Eskimo traditions of Alaska, personal names convey meaning. Nothing could be more personal than the names we call each other, and here again, there are stories. Sometimes we are named after someone special in our family. Sometimes, such as in Eskimo society, this means that we are expected to be like that person, to reflect their qualities, to carry on their lives in our life. In South Africa, a name may commemorate the events or actions at the time of our birth. My friend Zakes carries the name Phegello which means "perseverance." At the time of his birth there was a flood and the person who drove his mother to the hospital had to drive through floodwaters. The driver's perseverance will be remembered for as long as Zakes and his family tell this story.

Sometimes personal stories need a particular occasion to introduce them into the common lore of a community. At a Communities of Memory storytelling session in Kotzebue, Alaska, two Vietnam War veterans told their stories, and like the victims who told their stories for the Truth and Reconciliation hearings in South Africa, these vets said that they felt better after sharing their accounts. These were very personal narratives; they wanted their community to hear and know what they had experienced, to make their story part of what the community knows, part of the common lore. They spoke about the horrors of war and the things that they had been asked to do—killings and other acts of violence, experiences quite foreign to their family and neighbors in remote Alaska communities.

The Vietnam vets' stories were based on experiences they had thirty years ago, ones they had told to each other and to other vets, but that were not well known at home, not incorporated as part of the regional history. They told us that retelling their personal stories at this public setting helped them to work through the horror, to gain support from their community, and to reaffirm their sense of well-being.

The Vietnam vets' stories are quite different from the accounts we heard from their elders who served in World War II or their families who suffered hardships when the men went off to serve. In World War II, there was a common fear of attack from the enemy and a common understanding of the times. The community had a way to understand and place people's personal stories within the realm of shared experiences, whether the descriptions were of going off to Nome to join the service, going to a remote part of the state to build an airfield, or those of a young mother left home to provide food and care for her children.

Statues, Monuments, and Objects That Invoke and Represent Story

Sometimes stories are closely linked to objects. To mention or view an object is to conjure up images and experiences, and this often prompts us to share this meaning with others. In fact, we sometimes create special objects just to recognize, commemorate, and celebrate events and people.

In American history we speak of the Statue of Liberty as a gift from France to serve as a welcome sign for all who come to the shores of the United States seeking freedom and a new start. It is meant to remind us of our land of opportunity echoed in the many accounts of thankful immigrants. This story has taken on new meaning in recent years because of growing tensions over illegal aliens. These news stories compete with the image of our country welcoming newcomers, a nation built with the help of many national and ethnic groups from near and far. The stories and the meaning behind this and other monuments are not static—they evolve.

In a very different part of the world, the Vortrekker Monument in Pretoria, South Africa, represents, preserves, and stimulates story. The monument was built to document the history of Boers in South Africa and to publicly proclaim the belief that they have a chosen place in the land and in God's eyes. The monument is a massive, imposing structure surrounded by cement replicas of the wheels from the covered wagons that transported the Dutch settlers through the country. The interior frescos visually tell the history of the Boers, the leaders, the battles, and the signs they received from God.

Today, in modern South Africa, the monument stands as a memorial to proud pioneers who settled the country, to a way of thinking, to a time in history, and to a group of people whose vision of the world and their place in it created atrocities of racial prejudice that should never be repeated. It stands as an anomaly in the new South Africa, but as a prominent Black official from Johannesburg said in a newspaper article, which is surprisingly part of the display, the monument is important because it reminds us of a previous regime, a reminder of how things were, and how they should never become again. That was not the original intent of the monument, but for many, that is what it has become.

On King Island, in Alaska, there is a statue called Christ the King. It was brought to the island by Father Hubbard in 1937 (Renner and Ray 1979, 104–05). There are lots of stories about this shrine; it has become part of the place, part of a sense of King Island. Before the statue arrived, one of the islanders predicted Christ would come and would make his way up to where the statue now stands. In the oral tradition, the coming of the statue for some fulfilled that prophecy (Kingston 1999, 132). In this case, the shrine, for some, took on significance beyond the original intent.

There is tremendous power in sacred objects, whether they are large statues or small icons depicting church history and messages of faith. The importance of these objects to communities should never be underestimated. Anthropologist Nancy Davis reports that, after the 1964 earthquake, the people in Kaguyak on Kodiak scrambled for their lives onto high ground. They took with them some of the holy pictures and the icon of St. Nicholas, the patron saint of the village. They placed these holy items in front of them and they held a service. That's when the water from the tsunami began to retreat (1971, 106). After they were rescued, they asked the captain of the ship to stop in the bay where the wrecked church had landed. They were able to retrieve a large Easter icon (1971, 112, 273).

The importance of these religious objects is also illustrated by my friend Jill Holmgren, who recalls the story she heard of people in Sitka. When it was clear that fire would spread to the Russian Orthodox Church, they formed a bucket brigade to get the icons and crosses out of the church and to a safe place. The brigade wasn't limited to Russian

Orthodox parishioners, and when they were ready to re-establish the icons in the new church, they found that all of the sacred objects had been safely kept and returned. The irreplaceable nature of these objects and their importance to people gives them a value that can't be calculated in any material way.

Stories about the icons are interesting for at least two reasons: first, because they are the ancient church records of saints performing acts of mercy, kindness, and love; and second, because they speak to people today and help remind them of old church stories that can help them as they address problems in their lives. In the fall of 2000, graduate student Eugene Filipowicz interviewed several people about icons, and they told him stories about how the icons have been used in times of need. In this case, stories about the icons have become part of the oral tradition and are discussed. But the interesting thing that Eugene found is that the icons don't have to be discussed to continue to inform. For those who have heard the stories, the visual presence is often enough to remind them of the ancient sacred accounts and the more recent personal stories of how the icons address their needs. Objects both contain and represent story. In some cases, their very presence is the message.

Quilts are a very personal form of expression and they are rich in story. My friend and colleague Phyllis Movius points out that in many aspects of the American experience, women have used quilts to depict the social, political, and personal (1999, 111–12). One of the most interesting types of quilts is made from quilt squares prepared for parents who are grieving the loss of a baby. My quilting friends Colleen Jones and Phyllis Movius described to me how members of the local quilters group make these for the hospital to give to parents when their babies die. They are called Amanda quilts after a baby that was stillborn. The quilts replace disposable paper blankets. Some parents choose to bury their babies in the quilts; others keep them to help themselves through the grief. Also, some people make their own quilts as a way to work through personal loss. A friend shared with me how, when her mother was ill, she received a special gift. Her mother gave her buttons, bows, and some fabric. During her mother's illness my friend fashioned a vest from these materials. Her mother passed away at Christmas time, and now the daughter wears the vest each year at the holiday time as a way to remember her mother.

In other cases, quilts are made to celebrate an occasion, such as an adoption, a retirement, or a wedding. In each case, the act of creating

and the final display of the finished product become part of a partici-
patory creative process, a way to express meaning. The result is a story
of the event and the creative act that publicly recognizes and expresses
what it means to the quilter. The story is often unspoken, but the
meaning is known.

Recently, I purchased a deck of cards from a store in Dutch
Harbor, a center for fishing in the Aleutians. The cards feature the
crab fishing fleet that operates in Alaska. The cards owe their origin
to Mike Cramer, who made them in 1978. Each card features one of
the crab fishing boats. Cramer is quoted as saying, "I came up with
the idea because during the seventies we were on strike a lot, and a
lot of the time we'd sit around and play cards. I said, 'Gee, I should
have a deck of cards with all these boats on them.'" Jim Paulin, writing for the *Anchorage Daily News*, (Paulin 1999) goes on to point out
that a lot of these boats have undergone alterations over the years—
widening, addition of more mechanized gear—and some have sunk.
To those who worked on them, the cards are a reminder of a multitude of stories.

In Beaver, grave markers are carved with a symbol representing
how the individual is remembered: a trap for a trapper, a parachute
for an Army paratrooper, a gun for a marksman. The tradition probably goes back to a White trapper, Jay Eisenhart, who had a cabin in
Beaver for many years. One of his contributions was to carve the
grave markers.

In each of these cases, the objects have meaning because we have
learned enough to know the value of them and to know the stories
behind them. Barre Toelken tells about Evalina Matt, the Yurok bas-
ketmaker, who was hired to do a workshop on basketmaking. When
the students became impatient after many days of hearing songs and
then singing songs in the forest as they gathered plants, Matt told
them, "The songs are basic to basketmaking; after all, a basket is a
song that's been made visible" (1996, 189–90). The stories give
meaning to the objects and the objects then remind us of the stories
behind them.

Julie Cruikshank, in her work with Mrs. Kitty Smith, also explores
the power of objects to tell a story. Mrs. Smith was a carver who saw
in wood the potential to convey stories and so she carved. The
objects are in Julie's words, "illustrations for particularly meaningful
stories." Mrs. Smith had rich oral traditions to draw on, and carving
provided a way to visually retell the stories (Cruikshank 1998, 104).

We have a recent example of how clearly stories and objects are linked. After the crash of Alaska Airlines flight 261, on January 31, 2000, a story emerged about a Masonic ring that belonged to one of the victims, Bob Williams. There are actually four stories here, the father and daughter pact, the recovery of the ring, the daughter's interpretation of what it meant, and a friend's interpretation of what Bob Williams did to ensure it was recovered. Bob Williams' ring was recovered from the deck of a fishing vessel involved in the search for survivors. The ring was traced to Williams, and his daughter told the story of how she and her dad had a pact that each would try to inform the other of life after death. For Tracy Knicek, Bob's daughter, the ring was a tangible sign that her father was communicating to her, indicating that all was as they expected (*Fairbanks Daily News-Miner*, 4 February 2000). A friend of the family suggested that maybe Williams took the ring off and placed it in the seat cushion, thereby giving it the best chance of recovery (6 February 2000). To Tracy, this ring now means everything. It is a source of reassurance, a sign from her father. The ring and the stories represent a type of closure.

Stories can represent *inherited significance*—that is, there can be stories about objects that are passed down through the generations. They may hold *material value,* as in the clan crests and ceremonial regalia of Southeast Alaska Native groups. These are owned by the clans and each tells a story of the ownership, of authority and rights to confer title, and of significant events in the clan's history, events that engendered gift and recognition. Other objects, such as a family heirloom, may be significant because they belonged to someone special to us and seeing them brings back memories. The memories are often framed as stories.

My mother has a Hitchcock rocking chair[13] that has meaning to us because her great aunt gave it to her and this person was special in her life. The rocker has been passed down from my mother's great-great-grandmother to my mother's great aunt, and then to my mother. My mother's great-great-grandmother was given the rocker when she was a young woman by her husband. They came from Germany, and when they were expecting their first baby, the husband gave her the Hitchcock rocker to rock their baby. The heirloom has importance to us on several levels: the great aunt who inherited the rocker from her mother helped raise my mom and was very good to her. My mother's advanced education was made possible through a generous inheritance from that aunt. Ironically, the money came from a member of the Hitchcock family, Henry Hitchcock, someone great aunt Harriet nursed during his last years. He was very fond of my mother and wanted to help her. I grew up with his picture on the wall, a handsome man on horseback. The rocker has meaning for me because I know how important that great aunt was to my mother and the rocker reminds me of that point. Every family must have similar stories of inherited significance.

Objects can also be *purposefully created to convey meaning*, to tell story, as in Mrs. Smith's carvings or as in memorials to events and people, objects such as the monuments already mentioned.

Then there are objects that take on *expanded meaning as they prompt story*. I had the pleasure to be present in Unalaska when the dories exhibit opened. The exhibit was the idea of Maeve Doolittle, who owned the boats. Maeve acquired them in the Aleutians, gave them life for a while in Seattle, and now, thanks to her efforts and the efforts of others, they have embarked on a new life, back in the Aleutians, in the museum. The history of these boats is closely associated with Robert "Sea Otter" Jones who was a Fish and Wildlife Service agent. He traveled the rough waters of the Aleutian Islands in these open craft and did pioneering work to document wildlife in the Aleutians. Maeve's exhibit and the return of the boats to the Aleutians have been a stimulus for people to talk about the boats, about Bob Jones, and about their own experiences.

At the opening of the exhibit, people examined the boats in detail, told about how they handle, how they loaded them, how they traveled with a load, the value of outboards over inboards, beaching them in surf, and the differences between east and west coast dories. The boats are inspiring story and reflection on life in the Aleutians.

Sometimes games will inspire story. Yup'ik girls in Southwest Alaska practice "storyknifing." Using a bone or butter knife, they draw in the mud or snow and create picture stories. There are specific signs that represent objects and activities. Some of the stories are old and some are created at the moment (Ager 1971). In a somewhat similar way adults and children in the central Canadian Arctic play a game called *inugaq*, or "bone game." Seal bones are pulled out of a mitt and are used to construct activity areas. In this game, the different types of bones represent things such as animals, men, women, snow house walls, and seats in the snow house. By arranging the bones, they tell stories (Webster 1989).

When the Oral and the Literate Come Together

Of course, stories make their way back and forth between the oral and the literate. The book *Portraits in Steel*, a wonderful award-winning book by the photographer Milton Rogovin and the oral historian Michael Frisch, is about the experiences of steel workers in Buffalo, New York, a big steel manufacturing area on Lake Erie. One of the interviews that Michael Frisch did was with a single mom who started work in the steel mills to support her family. She helps us understand the struggles women face when they want to break into a profession dominated by men. We also get a fair dose of her spunky and quick-witted personality:

> The men resent the women for being there. There still was a resentment that the women were taking away the jobs from the men. So I just told them, I says, "I never really wanted to come here, you know, just nothing about this place excited me, but I was sent here." And I says, "You know, I have two children and when your kids go to the football games, mine'd like to go to them, too, and mine like those sneakers same just like yours. If somebody else was buying them, then all well and good," I said. "But my kids are no different than yours. If they had a father, or that man to be there to take care of them, I wouldn't be here! But since they're not there, I want to give them the same thing that you're giving yours." And from then on I never had any more problem out of them. (Rogovin and Frisch 1993, 185)

From one story, we can't tell whether her experiences and expression of concerns were typical of other female workers at the time, but the story opens one small window on one person's experiences. When combined with other people's stories, we can begin to appreciate what it was like for women to break into a traditionally male trade.

Another good example of this theme is Sherna Gluck's study of women aircraft plant workers during World War II. In *Rosie the Riveter Revisited* (1987), she interviewed many of the women who worked in this industry and elicited their stories of the work and the working environment. The study shows a wide variation in experiences and reasons why women joined the work force. Her interviews also traced the women's lives after leaving the industry.

One of the things the study showed was that this work opened up new opportunities for the women but that after the war ended, many of these doors of opportunity closed. There was a general attitude among many people that the women had met the crisis, and now that the men were back from war, the women should relinquish their jobs and return to the home. Nevertheless, Gluck concludes that the wartime experiences did help to broaden the horizons of women and contributed in a small but "incremental" way to the "tide of rising expectations of women" (Gluck 1987, 267–69). Similar themes are echoed by Laurie Mercier in her study of Anaconda, the Montana copper-producing community (Mercier, 2001).

In each of these cases—steel workers, aircraft workers, and copper producers—the oral record is particularly important because now these stories are not just part of the experiences of the women who told them and their circle of friends. Now they are part of a literature that is accessible to a wide audience of readers. But what does it mean to be part of a literate and oral tradition?

Writing can extend the message to a larger audience, but the act of telling and retelling fulfills human needs—a need of the tellers to make personal contact with others and a need by the audience to hear the narrator. Speeches and sermons are examples of how the spoken word continues to serve, in certain settings, as the primary and most effective way to communicate information. Literary readings are a good example of how writers find an effective way to disseminate their written work by combining it with an oral presentation.

Sometimes it is hard to tell where the oral ends and the written begins. My favorite example of this comes from Turak Newman and the story of the camp robber. Turak used to tell the story about the Yanert brothers who lived down at Purgatory on the Yukon River, about forty miles downstream of Beaver. One of the stories that he told was how the Yanerts had a mysterious grave at their place with a wooden marker that said something like "He stole from me so he met his Waterloo." When the tourists on the steamboat saw the grave and the inscription, they decided it should be reported to the United States marshal in Tanana. The marshal knew the Yanert brothers well and couldn't imagine any wrongdoing but felt obliged to investigate. So he visited their place, and in the dark of night he dug up the grave, only to find a small box with a camp robber (Canadian jay) inside. These birds are very bold and known for approaching food left unattended, hence their name. The Yanerts were waiting and watching the marshal as he dug up the grave and when he had it uncovered, the Yanerts lit a light and everyone had a good laugh.

For years, I thought this was a story that lived only in the oral tradition, possibly only as Turak's personal narrative. Years later, much to my surprise, I was shown a brochure from one of the steamboat companies that listed where they stopped and a little story about each place. There under Purgatory was the story of the camp robber. And it doesn't end there. Another friend, commenting on how much she likes travel books, passed on Rebie Harrington's 1937 account of travels in Alaska. I followed the index down the Yukon to Purgatory and there, to my pleasure and surprise, was a rendition of the same story (1937, 136–37). Now, I really don't know where the story originated. All I know is that it appears in the written and the oral traditions and that it is very similar to other stories about the Yanerts, who were great jokers (see Cruikshank 1986, 39–42).

Written and oral traditions can feed off each other, but unlike the written tradition, telling stories is a continual act of creation, of performance. Ruth Finnegan puts it well when she says, "Oral literature is by definition dependent on a performer who formulates it in words on a specific occasion—there is no other way in which it can be realized as a literary product. In the case of written literature a literary work can be said to have an independent and tangible existence in even one copy" (1970, 2).

Referring to performance in storytelling, Finnegan makes the point that this dynamic is what enables storytellers to choose settings for maximum impact, to create metaphor, to add emphasis, and to use rhythm to build dramatic and powerful meaning each time a story is told. She has fought against the tendency of scholars to reduce African stories purely to text and has continued to point out the literary value in the art of storytelling.

Greg Sarris makes a similar point. For many years Greg was a student of Mabel McKay, a California Pomo Indian who lived in the area around San Francisco. Greg came to realize that Mabel's stories were not static products or commodities but a continuous creative process of "negotiating" meaning. He writes, "Mabel does not end or close her story but opens it continually, by the dialogue she has both with it and with the person hearing it. Her story—her talk—counters literate tendencies that would close the vastness of its world and, hence, the complexity of its teller" (Sarris 1993, 47).

Earlier, Greg quotes Dennis Tedlock, who said, "The speaking storyteller is not merely addressing a hypothetical future audience, unlike the writer. The world evidenced by the audible text, considered in its entirety, includes not only the world projected by the story proper but the world of the performer and audience" (Tedlock 1983, 10).

This point was brought home to me recently when I asked Peter John for a quote we could use for the 1999 national Oral History Association meeting in Anchorage. We wanted to emphasize the importance of story and some of the complexities of understanding the meaning of story. Peter was in town to give a talk and I met him at his daughter's house. We discussed the program, then I quickly took notes as he talked. *"In between the lines is something special going on in their minds, and that has got to be brought to light, so they understand just exactly what is said."*

Like Mabel, Peter sees story as a creative play between teller and audience and between words and meaning—an incomplete fit that demands that we struggle to understand, to create common space, whether we are tellers or audience, speakers or writers, listeners or readers.

As in so many of the things Peter says, I am never quite sure whether I understand all that he means. I say this because sometimes I will be thinking about what he has shared and I'll understand more than was immediately obvious but will wonder if this is what he meant or what I am "reading" into it? In the above quote, I think "they" and "their" have double meanings, referring to the teller and to the audience. I also think Peter was using the word "lines" as a way to compare and contrast written and oral communication and to point out the need in both cases to get beyond the literal to deeper levels of meaning, to work through the gulf between the intended meaning of the teller/writer and the perception of the listener/reader.

In the oral tradition, the decision to tell a story and the way a story is told and understood is a dynamic process that involves continuous attention to "what is going on in their minds." Dialogue, response, and restating over a period of time in different settings and with different implied reasons for telling can give us the background to understand. Our interpretations get tested as we become familiar with the teller and how he or she uses story to "negotiate meaning" in each telling.

The notion that in oral tradition meaning is negotiated in the telling is commonly understood by folklorists (see for instance Bauman 1986), but I first came to see its utility when my colleague Jim Ruppert used the concept to describe how people at the Nome Communities of Memory meeting expressed their sense of identity as a community by choosing to tell particular stories. The process of telling stories to each other establishes with fellow community members a sense of how they see their community. What is so interesting about Nome is the fact that, beyond a common body of stories, there are stories by different subgroups: the pioneers, the Natives, and the new arrivals, to mention just a few. Will sessions like the Communities of Memory project help the community as a whole develop more of a common lore? Do they want a common lore? We don't know; the experiences of each group are quite different and important to them in their own way (Schneider 1998c).

People in Nome have gone on to create a book and video of the storytelling (Sabo 1997, 1999), so at least some people are interested in preserving the different stories in multiple ways. We now have the process of telling and hearing, and the artifacts of that, in the video and the book. Artifacts may seem like a harsh word, but a book and all recordings, audio and video, for better or worse, are static. They stand in isolation until the individual or a group of readers and listeners begins to relate the contents to their experiences and decides to retell the story. In the oral tradition there is give and take between the teller and his or her audience through many tellings (meaning is negotiated at each telling), but this is not possible in the written and recorded work—hence the value of discussions and experience as a way to determine meaning from what we have read in a book or heard on a tape. This has been a constant theme in Dennis Tedlock's work, where he encourages dialogue as a way to preserve a fuller record of how the narrator uses story to convey meaning and demonstrates how this can be done in the published text (Tedlock 1979, 1983, 1990). Of course, it is nice when we can go back to the author or the narrator and seek their clarification, but in the end, our understanding is based on how we make sense of what we have read or heard. Geertz would say that what is important is our ability to imagine the construct or universe in which the teller and audience share meaning (1973, 13).

Mabel McKay told Greg Sarris: "Don't ask me what it means, the story. Life will teach you about it, the way it teaches you about life" (1993, 5).

My colleague Dave Krupa reminded me that our interpretive work, whether we are audience, teller, reader, or writer, can and should be viewed as "a contemporary enactment of [the] human need for narrative and meaning." Overcoming our fears of "getting it wrong," we need to remember that without interpretation and retelling the story stagnates or, worse yet, is lost from memory.

Sorting Out Oral Tradition
and Oral History

I imagine that there were quite a few surprised people that day back in 1988 when Mrs. Angela Sidney retold the ancient Ḵaax̱'achgóok story at the dedication of the new Yukon College in Whitehorse. Ḵaax̱'achgóok had been lost at sea for a long time, blown off course and stranded on an island. He found ways to feed his crew and he carefully observed the sun, devising a sextant to plot the course of the sun. From this he was able to gain a sense of direction and navigate his way home. Mrs. Sidney, a distinguished Tlingit elder, told the people gathered at the dedication that she hoped the new college would give students a place to learn where they would be near and not separated from their homes. "The reason I sang this song is because that Yukon College is going to be like the sun for the students. Instead of going to Vancouver or Victoria, they're going to be able to stay here and go to school here. We're not going to lose our kids anymore. It's going to be just like the sun for them, just like for that Ḵaax̱'achgóok" (Sidney 1988, 9–16; also quoted from Cruikshank 1995, 69).

This was not the first time that Angela Sidney had told the story. She told it once when her son Pete returned from World War II. That time she sang the song to him as a gift. Like Ḵaax̱'achgóok, he had returned from afar after a long time (Cruikshank 1995, 67). Mrs. Sidney had told this story to Julie Cruikshank many times; it was a way that she could prepare Julie to understand how she used story to find meaning in her life (Cruikshank 1998). The story continues to be told; Julie retold it at the national Oral History Association meeting in Anchorage, October 8, 1999. Nora Dauenhauer told it the next day at the same meeting, and Bob Sam mentioned the day before Julie's telling that he is learning the story. Each draws meaning from this ancient story and each is trying to remind us of its meaning today.

I begin this discussion of oral tradition and oral history with Julie Cruikshank, Angela Sidney, and the Ḵaax̱'achgóok story because it illustrates how active a part oral tradition can play in guiding us about how to live and explain what's happening in our lives and to point to the wisdom of elders who used the ancient texts. Cruikshank and Mrs. Sidney's work also points to an appropriate role for oral history—to explain how the recorded story is used and the conditions for appropriate retelling and interpretation. Julie's essay is, after all, more than a reporting of the story—it is a discussion of how the story has been told, the occasions and the protocol that Angela Sidney followed. Our understanding of all the tellings enhances our appreciation for the way the story is used to convey meaning in a particular telling. I want to also note that Mrs. Sidney decided to publish a further explanation in the *Northern Review* (Sidney 1988) as a way to ensure fuller understanding of the story and how it was used at the dedication of Yukon College. In this way, Angela Sidney and Julie Cruikshank illustrate the main thesis of this book, that the oral record is an artifact of a telling and can only be understood and managed against the backdrop of many tellings in many different situations. We need the oral tradition to teach us about oral history and this story is a model for how it can be done. Unfortunately, we don't have the same amount of information for many stories; we haven't learned to ask, when have you told this story before? and why did you choose to tell it? Of course, these aren't easy questions to ask; most people don't keep track of when and why they tell a story, and most fieldwork isn't long enough to record enough of this information. But, these are the questions we need to address.

Oral Tradition

I define oral tradition as the stories that people tell, the ones they commonly know and consider important enough to pass on to future generations. The key variable is the act of people sharing common knowledge that they pass on to future generations. Because this base of knowledge is always being molded in new ways and because those who share it are continually changing, oral tradition is best considered an abstraction. It is a generalization about common understandings at different points in time.

Oral tradition is a useful concept in at least three ways: (1) It gives us a sense of what people know and choose to share with each other. (2) Over time, oral tradition provides a key to what and how people remember, forget, and form new understandings. This process of

remembering, forgetting, and forming new understandings sometimes takes place with the same people, sometimes with new groups.
We have to be very careful not to define common understanding too
rigidly because meaning and understanding is negotiated, produced,
and applied between people in different circumstances (see for
instance Morrow 1995, 27–51, for examples of just how difficult this
is). (3) Following David Cohen (1994), we also recognize that oral
traditions invite production rather than merely a recitation of history.
Angela Sidney comes from a culture imbued with respect for protocol, rules which she followed closely in her life, but she also saw
opportunities to use stories in new ways to create understanding and
bring meaning to events.

Implicit in my understanding of oral traditions is the assumption
that I can recognize a group of people who, to varying degrees and
at some points in time, not only know the stories, but also have common understandings of what the stories mean and how and when
they can and should be told. Part of the energy and power of story is
the room provided and expected for new understandings and appli-
cations. Testimony to this fact is the power and interest generated in
the K̲aax̲'achgóok story by storytellers at the Oral History conference. This is truly the "production of history."

We can see the process of applying story in the use of sayings that
speak to particular themes that are both historically important and
relevant to the present. In South Africa the term *ubuntu* has taken on
transcultural meaning and keeps producing new meanings over time
in different contexts.

Ubuntu is a Xhosa word that commonly translates as "a person is
a person through other persons." For Archbishop Desmond Tutu, the
term refers to a theological principle. If man is created in the image
of God, then we must all share something in common, our sense of
what it means to be part of the human family, sons and daughters of
God, who is the father (Battle 1995, 246–47). Archbishop Desmond
Tutu is often credited with making the term ubuntu popular throughout the country, and now it is heard beyond the borders of Africa.

I first remember hearing the term back in October of 1997 in the
dining room at the University of the North. I always looked forward to
lunch at UNIN. Africans eat later than Americans, and so I was always
hungry by then. The other and more important reason is that lunch
was often a good time to visit and for me to learn from my African
friends. On this occasion, they were explaining how it was traditional

for everyone to eat from the same dish and to drink beer from the same vessel. There is, they explained, a sense of relief from the anxiety over getting enough. The sentiment is that when we all eat or drink together (share), we become satisfied (filled up). That is ubuntu.

My next exposure to the term was a conversation during the fall of 1998 with Ethel Kriger, at that time the head of transformation at the National Archives in South Africa. Transformation refers to the efforts of the government and the society at large to develop democratic institutions and ways of operating. It refers to the making of constitutions and the establishment of workplaces that reflect the new democratic ideals. In this context, traditional phrases play a part in helping people to think about how they want the new government to be shaped. Ethel used the term ubuntu (or *umuntu*) to mean "an organizing philosophical principle, a construct to help South Africans focus around something (intrinsically?) good." That is, it allows people an opportunity to focus on the idea of common destiny and codependency (Kriger, personal communication, October 1998; see also Kriger 2001, 99).

The strength of ubuntu is its application in all of these settings, the fact that people can see its meaning as intrinsic to a range of experiences, old and new, social and political, philosophical, religious, and practical. Ubuntu has become many stories because it can be fruitfully applied to many settings, and it conjures up in people's minds a range of associations that have meaning. It has become transcultural, with people from many different backgrounds identifying and using it. For instance, I recently heard about "ubuntu video clubs," supported by the Rockefeller Foundation and the National Endowment for the Arts.

In the fall of 1999 my friend and colleague from the University of the North, Thoko Hlatywayo, related a similar saying that emphasizes the strong communal aspect of African society: "Children of the same mother share the same locust head." This saying means that family members share with each other, no matter how little they have. When I asked Thoko about the origins of the expression, she said it was northern Sotho, but it is also known in other languages. She went on to relate a Zulu expression that a traveler might use when approaching strangers for a place to spend the night: "A stranger's stomach is very small; it is equal to that of a bird's kidney." She explained it is like saying that I am hungry and require just a little bit of food. Of course, the stranger would be lodged and fed, even given food for the trip. To Thoko, this is an example of ubuntu.

The story of ubuntu continues to unfold. On my last trip to South Africa I purchased a deck of cards, The African Renaissance Deck, that features symbols of "uBuntu": pots to represent nourishment, shields for standing up to adversity, huts for adequate housing, and beads to convey emotion (African Wisdom Creations 2000).

South Africans actively share adages, sayings, and proverbs to convey meanings that are universally important. In some cases, this is a concerted effort to draw upon the oral tradition to find meaning in the present and for the future. We see it in prominent figures like Archbishop Desmond Tutu, in institutions like the South African Broadcasting Company, and in efforts of the South African government. South African Broadcasting has picked up the term *simunye*, which means "we are one," and it is broadcast much like a commercial with actors from different parts of the population participating in the statement.

In October 1997, the government issued a white paper, Notice 1,459, titled *Batho Pele* (a Sesotho expression for "people first") that is a call for public servants to use the adage as a theme to guide how they do their work and relate to the public. The goal in all these efforts is to reinforce a common tradition, a "public culture" that can nourish the new nation. They are doing this by drawing on the richness of the oral tradition.

When most people think of oral tradition, their reference is not to such phrases but to myths and legends, things like the Kaax̱'achgóok story. When I think of myths, my reference is to stories that are so old that no one can trace direct relationship to the characters or events. They may involve actions that are foreign to our experiences or how we know the world works, such as stories of giant fish that can swallow kayakers who try to cross lakes in the Brooks Range of Alaska (Burch 1971). Myths often contain a moral teaching or explain the origin of a prominent feature.

When I think of legends, my reference is to those old accounts of important figures or events traceable to a particular time or person. Often legends grow larger and more significant as we recognize how the characters and events relate to present circumstances or represent important themes. (Note that these definitions differ somewhat from those offered by Isidore Okpewho [1992, 182–83], and my point in offering them is not to strictly define but to broaden the basis of our discussion.)

Legends often center on folk heroes such as Mauneluk, the great Eskimo prophet who lived on the Kobuk River in Northwest Alaska and predicted many of the events and changes that have taken place and defied traditional taboos (Sun 1985, 7–13 and Giddings 1961, 31–34). The nonprofit social organization for the region is now called Mauneluk after the great man. I also think of the Zulu warrior chief Shaka, bigger than life in the recall and portrayal, traceable in time and place to a real person and real events. This character has generated incredible historical attention and public notoriety in print, on screen, and even on the Internet. Just what do the modern stories of Shaka represent? What do they tell us about the interests and concerns of people today? Shaka was a great military leader; his exploits reshaped the population of South Africa and influenced the politics of all of southern Africa. Now, for the Natal region, he is a symbol of Inkatha and the leadership role they would like to play in the modern South Africa (Hamilton 1998).

The interesting thing about these folk heroes is that they prod us to ask why they remain important; what satisfaction do people get out of talking about them, portraying them in song and film, or in naming organizations after them? Part of the answer lies in an observation by Edward "Sandy" Ives, a folklorist and student of backwoods Maine culture. In his book on George Magoon (*George Magoon and the Downeast Game War,* 1998) Ives makes the point that folk heroes provide an opportunity for people today to identify with a person who has been able to achieve something that we would like to achieve. In the case of George Magoon, stories about him relay how he was kind of a Robin Hood figure, outsmarting the "misdirected" government and rich sport-hunter types and feeding the people with moose meat. Even if people don't benefit materially today from his exploits, they can appreciate his defiance of the law in defense of a greater good, and so they keep telling the stories.

Mauneluk is important because of his ability to predict, a rare power, in a sense more significant than all the technological changes that he foresaw. This type of power is unusual, but there are other historic figures in Alaska and the Yukon who we remember because they had powers that the newcomers (Whites) did not. In a sense, they represent successful opposition to the new forces and so are remembered at least partly in this light. (For a discussion of a powerful shaman from Herschel Island, see Nagy 1991a and b and 1994, 30–32. For discussion of the famous Yukon Flats chief Shahnyaati, see Schneider 1976, 315–27.) These figures are important because they tell us what people think went on in the past, but their historical significance is also linked to what people continue to value and how they choose to keep the oral tradition alive.

It is easy to forget that oral traditions are kept alive by the people because they speak to their needs and concerns. One of the students that I had the pleasure of knowing at UNIN is Amos Makhubele. On several occasions he shared stories with me. One time he said that he had a story that he wanted to tell me, an account from his grandmother. It was on his mind and had been the subject of conversations with a friend who also knew the story. Amos called this "The Story of Little Big Man." Amos remembers his grandmother telling it to him around the campfire at night. It is about a young man who is being prepared to journey to another village to marry. He is warned not to eat any of the fruit along the way. On his journey he is tempted and does eat the fruit. When he reaches his future wife's village, he is possessed with the Little Big Man. The wife's people can sense this and the marriage is called off (Makhubele 1997).

When Amos first heard the story, he didn't know what his grandmother was trying to tell him, but now, prompted to think and talk about stories, and in discussions with a friend who had also heard this story, he is prepared to offer an explanation. Amos says that the story is about AIDS and how this young man contracted the disease from women along the way to his future wife's village. Succumbing to temptation, the boy ruins his life, a familiar theme and even a familiar series of events, reminiscent of the biblical Garden of Eden. We don't know if this is the meaning that his grandma meant to convey, but the story remains important because Amos sees the story as a reminder of an important lesson. The story and how he made sense of it is now part of how he represents himself to me and presumably to others too.

On three public occasions, I heard Bob Sam, a young Tlingit man, tell traditional Tlingit stories. One of the stories that he tells is the story of "The Cannibal and Mosquito," sometimes called "The Cannibal and the Giant." The story is well documented as part of Tlingit oral tradition. (It is sometimes called simply "Mosquito" [see Dauenhauer and Dauenhauer 1987, 73–81 and 318–22]. At the University of Alaska Fairbanks, we even have a totem pole that tells the story, a forty-nine

foot totem carved in 1963 by Amos Wallace and erected in 1967 to celebrate the university's fiftieth anniversary.) What makes this story particularly important to Bob is that it was told to him by A. P. Johnson, a
respected elder who thought the story would help him. At that time,
Bob was a recovering alcoholic, and this old man had been watching
him closely and wanted to help. I don't have the rights to retell the
story, but like Amos' story, I can give a basic outline and point out
where I know it has been told: There was a cannibal who was destroying villages, eating people. A young man saw his family and fellow villagers destroyed, and he sought the power to rid the land of the
cannibal. He was given power but warned that he must not show
revenge or anger toward this terrible creature. He succeeds in killing
the cannibal, burns the body, and in a rage, blows on the ashes. The
sparks from this last act become mosquitoes, which are released into
the air as a lasting reminder of how he broke his promise and lost control of his emotions.

To some people, the mosquitoes represent alcohol, which is killing
the people, "sucking the life blood of the Tlingit" (Dauenhauer 1987,
319), and is hard to control. Bob explained that the cannibal is alcohol: "these monsters never go away; we can always fight them if we
remember where we get our strength" (Sam 1999). Now when Bob
tells the story (the three hearings I experienced), he recounts how old
A. P. Johnson used the story to remind him not to give in to temptation and to deal with adversity and temptation. Bob is a masterful storyteller who performs internationally. These stories are some of the
ways he actively shares his traditions with a wide range of audiences
(Sam 1998).

Like Amos, Bob sees a direct connection between the oral tradition, as reflected in this and other stories, and the development of
his life. The stories help these men to define their value system and
are vivid reminders of the elders who used oral tradition as a way to
speak to the younger generation. In a television interview, Bob said,
"we plant seeds," his way of pointing out how the meaning of stories
takes time to germinate and demands the proper conditions.

Often our personal stories are linked to the oral tradition. When
John Tsebe, the head of the UNIN library, introduced me to the cam-
pus, he drove me by the dorms and pointed out that they were named
by the students after political leaders they thought were important.
For instance, there are the Goddaffe House, Desmond Tutu House,
Martin Luther King House, and Shaka House, to name a few. I should

quickly point out that these are the only buildings on campus that are named. Only the streets in the staff residential area are also named, after influential members of the old apartheid government. The naming of the student dorms was an act of defiance against the administration and a statement of who the students admire (Housing Central Executive Committee 1993).

In a library science class, I mentioned to the students that I had learned that many of the dorms are named for people who were politically active in the fight against apartheid, and then I asked them if they knew any of the stories about these people and how the names were chosen. One lady volunteered that when she moved into the Samora Machel House, she was asked by a political activist if she knew about the person for whom the house is named. When she said she didn't, he told her about him. Her retelling of the story has particular meaning to her now because the student who told her it is no longer living. In this case, the oral tradition has been personalized by this woman's experience, which is now, for me, part of a bigger story that is unfolding about the role of the campus and students in the fight against apartheid.

Personal Narratives

In my work, it is helpful to differentiate oral tradition from personal narratives, although, as we will argue in the next chapter, personal narratives are integral to the formation and perpetuation of oral tradition. Personal narratives are stories that individuals tell about their experiences or observations, such as eyewitness accounts of disasters or the role they may have played in some event deemed worthy of recall. The woman who learned about Samora Machel shared her personal narrative, which built upon the oral tradition and expanded the importance of the naming. My sense is that much of oral tradition begins as personal narrative and makes the big leap to tradition when it is accepted by people as worthy of recall and retelling.

When we elicit life stories (Titon 1980), we ask people to use their personal stories to tell us about their lives. Often we get personal narratives such as where the person was born, where they lived, and what they did. Sometimes these narratives are interspersed with oral tradition. I suspect that Bob Sam might choose to tell the story I summarized above as a way to relate to others how his life was shaped by an elder's wisdom.

In unusual cases, the oral tradition will actually dominate a life story, as we see in Julie Cruikshank's work with women elders like Angela Sidney in the Yukon Territory of Canada. There, the life stories she collected tended to focus heavily on the oral tradition, on the old stories that helped these elders define their lives and the values they live by. The elders didn't want to talk about themselves, tell their personal narratives, until they felt that Julie understood the role of the old stories and embraced their concept of "Life Lived Like a Story" (1990). So, in many ways, oral traditions can frame and inform our understanding of personal narratives.

Oral History

Oral history consists of those parts of oral traditions and personal narratives that get recorded, that become a record. Oral history is both the act of recording and the record that is produced. This definition differs from others (Ritchie 1995, 1; Skotnes 1995, 66 and perhaps Portelli 1997, 5–6). These are scholars who see the interviewer as a critical part of producing an oral history record. I argue for a broader definition, which includes gatherings to tell stories, speeches, hearings, and testimonies. These settings often do not have a person asking questions. The Alaska Humanities Forum's Communities of Memory project is an excellent example of recordings produced from storytelling in Alaska communities and worthy of archival preservation, a record that should be accessible to the public for many years to come. We could also point to the Yukon International Storytelling Festival in Canada (Cruikshank 1998, 138–59) and the testimonies shared by South Africans during the Truth and Reconciliation Hearings.

There may not be an actual interviewer present asking questions, but if accounts are recorded and preserved in a public archive, there will be people using the record in various ways. Don Ritchie makes the important point that in these situations, the role of an interpreter is critical—someone who was present at the tellings and took the time to create a record of what went on and what prompted particular discussions, someone who can shepherd the recordings into a useful form for future users. Unfortunately, such a presence is rarely the case, unless plans are made to produce proceedings.

Once recorded, whether there is an interviewer or not, the narrative is separated from the speaker and their audience and is no longer subject to individual or community influences. However, understanding remains dependent on the interpretations of interviewers, narrators, and communities. The speakers and their audiences serve the important collective role of correcting, elaborating, and redefining. The recording without the narrators and tradition bearers is like a ship without a pilot. Verne Harris said it well when he noted, "The recording of narrative, the archiving of orality, can so easily destroy the fluidity, destroy the contextual links, alienate the speaker from the word. And the attempt to give voice to the voiceless ironically becomes a reinforcement of voicelessness" (1997a, 14).

I would like to engage Alessandro Portelli and Verne Harris on this point because in Portelli's definition of oral history, the writer/historian plays a vital role as interpreter. He states, "In the end, we might define oral history as the genre of discourse which orality and writing have developed jointly in order to speak to each other about the past" (1997, 5). Certainly we write about oral history as a way to communicate history, but a written rendering of stories is not always our goal, nor necessarily the best way to convey meaning. The first responsibility is, in Elizabeth Tonkin's terms, to "understand how history-as-lived is connected to history-as-recorded" (1994, 12). Then the thing to do is to find the best way to convey that understanding to others in the present and for the future. In some cases, writing is the best way. Certainly, the work of John Miles Foley (1995) is an example of how classical scholarship can preserve meaning in ancient texts that are based on oral narrative. Without such scholarship, the texts would be devoid of the voice and sentiment of ancient speakers and their audiences. Similarly, the work of Dell Hymes and Dennis Tedlock to preserve narratives in text form is important both in terms of preservation of meaning as well as for advancing method and theory.[14] That said, I am also reminded of Elsie Mather's warning that writing is a "necessary monster" (1995, 20).

For Elsie, the human link is what invites story. Storytelling is a key to relationships, values, and memory. While reading may inspire someone to seek out a storyteller, it can never substitute for the telling that comes when a storyteller chooses to share a story with you. Writing can preserve and interpret and even influence new tellings, but it must never frame the oral record as a fixed entity isolated from other tellings.

The challenge is to recognize how stories are used and to try to preserve the intended meaning as part of the recorded account. First there is the event that is described, and then there is the story that is told at a particular time about the event. The story that is told is subject to lots of different influences. Richard Bauman builds on Roman Jakobson's distinction between "narrated event" and "narrative event," the event that is described and the act of describing the event (1986, 112). This distinction lays out two crucial approaches to understanding narration: development of methods and means to record, analyze, and present texts (the ethnopoetics) and the methods and means to record and analyze the actual telling of stories (the performance). These two approaches are not exclusive, and the scholars just referenced seek to integrate the dimensions so to understand both what the story means and the ways it is delivered to communicate meaning.

Implicit in this discussion, is what Phyllis Morrow, following Michel Foucault, has termed, "the authoring function." This is the power that the compiler/recorder/writer assumes when he or she works with a narrator's story (Morrow 1995, 31) This is also part of the monster that Elsie refers to, the danger of a story leaving the culture and thereby becoming subject to manipulation and distortion. It is also Tonkin's point about the dangerous transition from story as told to story as recorded. It is why oral tradition and the community of people who share the tradition are so critical to our work; they are the lighthouse in the storm, and collaborative research is the hallmark of modern scholarship (see Evers and Toelken 2001).

In oral tradition, the narrating of an event is controlled by the narrator and listeners who choose to retell the story. Control rests further, though, with the individual narrator and his or her group, who decide how the stories are to be told, when, and to whom. This can be a formal process, as with Northwest Coast Indian stories that are owned by clans, but in most cases, for most groups, the process is informal and follows flexible conventions with lots of room for the teller to decide how he or she wants to use stories. Greg Sarris found that Mabel McKay would not let herself be recorded because she didn't want to be absent from any "discussion of her world" (1993, 23). I had a similar experience years ago when I visited an elderly lady at the Denali Center, a care facility in Fairbanks. The woman came from a family that was very active up in the gold diggings of the Koyukuk. I thought she would be an ideal person to tell me about the way people used horses to pull scows up the shallow river. When I asked her to tell me about it she refused to answer because she said that I didn't know enough to understand what she could tell me. This always impressed me as a good example of how narrators choose their audiences and of the importance of the background of the audience to understanding and perpetuation of tradition. In this case, she did not want an oral history record that might be misunderstood and misinterpreted.

If a story is not told and fades from memory, that represents a tacit decision by the group either that the story is not important enough to be part of the oral tradition or that they do not want to pass the information on to others. Sometimes a group will purposely decide not to continue telling a story or a type of story. In Alaska, stories of shamans are not commonly told publicly because missionaries heavily discouraged shamanism and people not only have chosen not to practice it but consider it a dangerous topic to even discuss.

There are some qualifications that can be made to my distinction between oral tradition and oral history. I have approached the subject from the standpoint of cultural groups who choose to tell their stories, including ancient oral narratives that they have retained and recount. What relation, though, do those stories that have been forgotten or are only partly remembered have to oral tradition? As noted, how they come not to be told anymore is a dynamic process subject to conscious and unconscious decisions about what will be remembered, how it will be told, and a range of implied meanings. But John Miles Foley and other classical scholars would question my tidy picture of what is part of oral tradition. They may ask, what about classical Greek stories that were written down, are no longer told orally, but are known and understood by scholars, who have discovered through research the context of the original tellings, the way words were used to convey specific meanings, and the use and placement of devices such as repetition to emphasize certain points? Can we say that these accounts are part of an oral tradition? In the sense that there is the potential to hear the oral structure and determine the generic meanings of these texts, I can see them acting like oral traditions and the community of scholars as a "cultural group." I hesitate, though, because there is not a surviving group of tellers who determine how the ancient texts continue to be used to reinforce *their* heritage and *their* sense of group identity. Of course, this does not exclude the possibility that some of the stories will reenter the oral tradition, in the sense that I use the term. For instance, stories from the Holy Bible and other religious texts are often incorporated into the narrative repertoire of believers, and they take on interpretive and performative dimensions. Most important, believers choose to retell and pass on the stories to future generations.

Summary

In all cases, the result of oral history is a recording that must be managed. Management involves preservation and access. Preservation includes more than keeping it from physical deterioration; it involves efforts to preserve the meaning expressed by the narrators and to adhere to their concerns about how it should be used. And, as we have noted, it also means placing the account within a framework of other tellings, at the minimum referencing those tellings.

Once the narrator stops talking and the recorder leaves with the tape, the teller no longer knows who will hear it and how they will understand what he or she said. This is why I find it helpful to use oral tradition as a guide to management of oral history. As we have already seen, this isn't always easy. Oral tradition changes; the concerns and issues of narrators and their home communities also change. To be fair to them and future users, we have to be mindful of a wide range of considerations, not the least of which is the oral tradition from which the narrator may have built the telling and from which the audience derives its background for understanding what has been shared. This is where the scholarship of academics and the knowledge of elders can come together to provide a fuller and more meaningful record. As Michael Frisch points out in his aptly titled book, *A Shared Authority*, the oral history endeavor must involve all contributors and the writer-author is but one of the players (Frisch 1989; Kline 1996).

Left to right, Julie Cruikshank, Catherine McClellan, and
Angela Sidney. Photo by Bill Ferguson, October, 1981.

Types of Stories

Personal Narratives
Shared One to Another

As one heads south from Pietersburg in the Northern Province of South Africa a mountain appears in the distance. On one of my first trips out of town, Zakes told me that was where Ernest Mothapo was born. Ever after that we joked about the place and how Ernest might retire there someday. My image of the place changed drastically a few months later when Zakes, Kgabi, Ernest, a few others, and I were sitting around the lunch table.

Kgabi Chuene was telling Zakes what a poor idea it was for him to buy a house in Potgietersrus, what a big commute it would be to work (45 minutes to an hour). As I recall, I then said something about people needing to be near their roots, and, by way of example, I mentioned Ernest's mountain. We were all shocked by what followed.

Ernest told us that it once was a German Lutheran Mission. His family was living there, and he was away at boarding school when he got a letter saying that they had been relocated from the site. Apparently the government bought out the missionaries and moved all the families out. (In a later conversation, Ernest clarified that it was government policy to take over schools, part of a total strategy to control education). They had to leave their cattle, sell them to the government, since, as the authorities explained, the new site would not be good for cattle. The new place was located just beyond Seshego, in a village under control of a chief. When Ernest first arrived there, walking on foot from the boarding school, he had no way to tell which house belonged to his parents. They all looked alike. The families provided their own corrugated metal to build shelters, and there were no provisions made for outhouses.

Ernest's relocation story is told from the perspective of a school boy, shocked at the news, disoriented by how to get to the new village, confused about how to find his family's house, and confronted by a new home that, reflecting back some thirty or forty years later, was far inferior to the one his family left at the mission near the big mountain south of Pietersburg.

I am conscious of how lean my retelling is in this written form compared to the impact of the story that day. Ernest's story is more than a piece of information about apartheid. His telling is a personal extension of his life that he chose to share with us on that day. My retelling pales because it is his story to tell in his way, and the moment he picked to share it held meaning for all of us sitting around the table. Now, I am trying to keep that meaning alive, but it is a different moment and you, the new audience, bring a different understanding to this moment.

The challenge of going from the original telling to a retelling is not unique to oral narratives. Alaskan writer Jean Anderson notes both writers and tellers work to extend story into new settings. She says we work with "secondhand talk," a gloss for all that is entailed when we recreate a story for a new audience (Anderson 1999). I think her expression "secondhand talk" is particularly appropriate from an audience's standpoint because, as listeners, we may become tellers in the future and our audiences will then be hearing secondhand. They may wonder how we know what we are saying. The challenge is for the reteller to introduce the story with enough background so that they communicate both the story and why they are retelling it then.

Ernest's story was told against the backdrop of our comments about Zakes's new house, a handsome place with all the amenities one could ever ask for, in a neighborhood with tree-lined streets and a park where kids can play. The contrast may not have been intentional, but the two images, one of prosperity and the good life, the other of hardship and repression, keep juxtaposing themselves in my mind and reinforcing the sadness of Ernest's account. That's the art and interest in storytelling; the teller chooses the moment, but the story dances in the experiences of the audience, reflecting off what they know and what was said before, against the site of the telling and the relationship of the people present (Schneider 1995b).

I was shocked by Ernest's telling because I had visited Zakes's township (the place where his mom and mother-in-law now live). I had also visited many of the houses and neighborhoods where he wanted to buy. I saw the disparity in wealth and comfort. When Ernest began his story, his reference to the mountain and their life there, a life filled with pleasant memories, caught my imagination and reminded me that we had earlier joked while driving near that mountain how Ernest would retire some day and build a casino there. There were other images too, of Sheshego, the township near where Ernest's family was forced to relocate. These were formed during a driving tour led by John Tsebe, the library director. He wanted me to see firsthand how the Afrikaner government had geographically segregated the population by color and ethnic characteristics. So, in my head, I was bouncing back and forth between my newly formed images: economically lean township versus luxurious suburb and beautiful mountain village versus destitute refuge camp. These contrasts were reflected against the legacy of a strict geopolitical engineering that John Tsebe had taken time to show me.

I remember and retell stories like Ernest's for several reasons. First, they tell about a part of the big event that I hadn't considered (reactions and perspectives of a school child to apartheid). Second, they are spotlighted by a present circumstance that makes them stand out (the disparity in wealth and opportunity between Zakes in 1997 and Ernest forty years before). Third, they present imagery that becomes imprinted in my mind (the big mountain and countryside next to the super highway, the quiet suburb of Potgietersrus where Zakes bought a house, and the nearby township where he grew up and where his mother and mother-in-law still live, a place rich in social ties but economically depressed).

In the following sections, I want to elaborate on these three points: the untold dimension, the present reminding us of the past, and the role of vivid imagery.

The Untold Dimension

Personal narratives often tell a part of a big story, filling in an important dimension that isn't commonly known or a part that just hasn't been highlighted. The best example I know from Alaska is the story Tishu Ulen told about her father, who was a hunter. Tishu was an elderly Inupiaq woman who grew up in the Brooks Range of north central Alaska. Her father hunted for moose and caribou, which he sold to the gold miners in the Wiseman area. Before I heard her story, I thought I knew about meat hunters, but I had not considered that, while they were often men, they were part of a family that had its own needs to be met. Tishu told how her mother followed her husband and set up camp, managing the dogs and caring for the children. In this case my knowledge of the functional unit and what it took to be a hunter was expanded in a very significant direction by Tishu's story. When you think about how difficult the woman's job was, particularly in winter, the man's part seems easy. The problem is that when we think about meat hunters, few of us think about women.[15]

> See, he goes ahead, like in the morning,
> he starts out.
> And she comes with the dog,
> four dogs, and two kids she had
> in the sled.
> She drive it, and she pitch the tent
> and get the fire going.
> The kids are crying (laughter)
> hungry!
> She make out though.
>
> (Tape H91-30-01, Oral History Collection,
> Elmer Rasmuson Library)

When I hear or read about meat hunters, I now think of Tishu Ulen and the woman's side of the story.

The Present Reminding Us of the Past

We often say that the past illuminates the present, but it works the other way too. Present events can remind us of a story from the past, thus bringing into focus both times. I remember that when Moses Cruikshank would meet with government people on land issues or attend other meetings, his contribution would often include a story from his prospecting days, the "pick and shovel days" is the way he put it.

One time, on an evening in 1974 at the old school in Beaver, there was a meeting called by a representative from the Joint Federal-State Land Use Planning Commission to gather input for national interest land proposals. The proposals contained the government's plans for management of large areas of Alaska. Moses asked the government representatives if mining would be allowed under the new land designations. When the officials mentioned restrictions, it provided a natural entrée for Moses to launch into a story about how he prospected all over the Interior. He wasn't talking about moving D-9 Cats into the country. For those of us from the community who knew Moses and his stories, the contrast between a law designed to stop big-time operators and the type of prospecting Moses did was strikingly clear. I'm quite sure that the officials did not understand Moses' plea. For us, the present was a sad reminder that the days that Moses talked about so fondly were gone, in part because of the difficulties of enacting legislation that would accommodate pick and shovel operations and yet limit the big earth movers.

On one of the North Slope projects, the government's outer continental shelf oil exploration program contracted with us to interview Inupiat regarding their involvement in oil exploration activities. The goal was to assess present concerns in preparation for exploration activity off shore. It was quite striking to me how Inupiat experiences from the 1940s had a profound impact on their concerns about environmental pollution.

The elders had experienced onshore oil exploration and could not imagine a man-made structure that would withstand the force of offshore ice when it decides to move. Their observations were based on what they had seen of the technology years ago and the stories they were raised with about the dangers of ice.

Most of the elders grew up hearing stories about people caught out on the ice and carried away. The tremendous power of the ice was a reality they grew up with. The experiences of individuals and the stories of their parents were the basis for informing and shaping their attitudes. I remember that in the village of Nuiqsut, in the corporation offices, there was a magazine with an advertisement from an oil company stating how they had extensively tested their drilling platforms at their laboratories in Texas to simulate the pressure of the ice on the North Slope. The contrast between the two types of knowledge was striking to me: the Inupiaq reference to personal experience and story and the scientific reference to controlled experiments, hundreds of miles away from the Arctic environment.

Our interviews were done in the early eighties, and since then many Inupiat have experienced modern oil development. I suspect that the gulf between Inupiaq personal narratives and oil company claims may not be so wide today, except, of course, in the case of elders too old to participate in modern oil development but well informed about ice (Kruse et al. 1983).[16]

Vivid Imagery

In Ernest's story we have a good example of vivid imagery—the corrugated metal houses that all look alike. These ubiquitous artifacts of the apartheid regime symbolically frame our image of the young boy walking along the road in search of his family's place. But how many of us have seen such structures?

For vivid imagery to work we have to be able to imagine the setting. For instance, long before I met Richard Frank, an Athabascan leader, I saw his picture, taken at a hearing in which he explained the impact of a road to the Minto Flats (Arnold 1976, 101). The Minto Flats border Fairbanks, and they are the traditional hunting grounds of the Minto people. Old Minto village is located on the Tanana River, about thirty miles from Nenana by trail. The new village of Minto is located on a spur road, off the highway to Manley Hot Springs. When I interviewed Richard, I had driven to new Minto, so I had part of the geography in my mind. After I visited Old Minto by dog team from Nenana and made a trip by boat from Fairbanks down the Chatanika River, I could imagine even more how close the traditional hunting and fishing grounds of the Minto people are to town. My experience helped me to understand what Richard was saying and to better sense the community's concerns over the road.

Since the community has moved from Old Minto and few people travel the trail from the old village to Fairbanks, I don't think that most young people can imagine the distances and the terrain, nor the extent of concern.

For years I have thought about a series of stories from Tanana, Alaska—accounts that emphasize experience. One of them was from Effie Kokrine, who told a story about George Edwin with love and appreciation for the old man and how he worked for the church: "I always remember, he put his hand in his pocket and he'll have dollars. We didn't have no dollar bill that time. He'd always drop his money into the plate, and in those days we were so poor that we had ten cents for offering and that was a sacrifice to give that ten cents. And he always put his dollar, 'clink'" (Tanana Elders, Recording H95-47, Oral History Collection, Elmer Rasmuson Library).

I have some silver dollars because my uncle used to give them to me for birthdays, so I have a sense of their size and weight and can imagine what they would sound like when they hit a metal offering plate, but can young people imagine this in the same way? Can I imagine how poor people in Tanana were at that time and the level of sacrifice George made in his contribution to the church? The image is vivid to Effie because she was poor, was there, and knew George. Good stories like Effie's give us just enough information to imagine. Sometimes these images stick with us; sometimes they come back to us later in life. Personal narratives are full of images, vivid to the elders but often based on experiences quite foreign to young people. Good storytellers stretch us to imagine, picture, and incorporate in our memory what they say. If a story sticks, then the images will come back to us in a vivid way and enrich us at different times.

Art of the Moment Crafted from the Past

Barbara Allen Bogart, a folklorist who has contributed immeasurably to my understanding of oral history, reminds us that everyone makes stories out of their experiences (Allen 1988, 21), choosing out of the myriad of possibilities which things to share in story and how to say it. The American folklorist Sandra Stahl defines personal narrative as "a prose narrative relating a personal experience; it is usually told in first person and its content is nontraditional" (1977, 20). For people we know well, we can predict what they will say in a particular situation and how the stories will be told. The personal choices are not, of course, made in isolation; they are predicated on the setting, the audience, and their interest and understanding. For these reasons, skilled storytellers find ways to bridge their "old" experiences to the younger generation; it's an art—call it art of the moment crafted from the past.

When members of the audience choose to retell a story, they give the engine the first crank to start it on the road to tradition. Much of oral tradition begins with, is built of, and depends on personal narratives, but the personal narrative is also most vulnerable to loss from generation to generation. If others pick up the story and retell it, the account becomes part of the oral tradition, but that does not always happen. Just as a personal narrative is a selection of what a person knows and represents how they wish to express their knowledge, oral tradition is an even finer filter of what the group knows. Only the most important or most interesting information is passed on by the group from generation to generation.

My colleague at the University of the North, Kutu Mphahlele, recently brought to my attention an article by H. O. M. Iwuji that quotes Vaillancourt Wagner: "Chaque viellard qui meurt, c'est une

bibliotheque qui brule (Each old man who dies, signifies the burn-
ing of one library)" (Wagner quoted in Iwuji 1990, 56; see also
Amadi 1981, 140). When Kutu shared this quote with me, I was surprised because I have heard people in Alaska use similar words to
express loss of an elder. Then, as I was reading Mary Pipher's book
Another Country, I ran across the quote again (1999, 11), this time
attributed to Alex Haley. My colleague, Molly Lee tracked the reference down (Haley 1976, vii–viii).

I'm not sure where the expression originated, but it needs a qual-
ifier. On face value, we can agree with the sentiment, particularly as
it relates to personal narratives. When an elder dies, we lose some of
their personal narrative and we lose a teller of the oral tradition. But,
the commonly known body of knowledge, what we have called the
oral tradition, depends not on one individual but on a group of
people who know it as the lore of the group and who share it at
appropriate occasions. So we can say that with the death of an elder,
we lose an important teller of oral tradition and, as was recently
pointed out to me by a group of graduate students, we also lose that
elder's particular relationship to the oral tradition, his or her ways of
using it and relating it to others. But hopefully there are others who
can and will also tell the story, even though the depth of knowledge
and ability to relate the story to others may pale compared to the
elder's telling.

Loss is inevitable, but artful use of the past to speak to the present doesn't end when an elder dies. In fact, the way we generate personal narratives and the way we use them to create meaning for the
moment is as important as their preservation for the future.

The ability to shape experience into story and to relate that story
to others for a desired effect is a distinctly human quality and is key
to our understanding each other. Verne Harris put it well when he
said, "Humans need story to make sense of their lives" (personal communication, September 1, 2000). Barbara Allen Bogart reminds us
that in the oral interview process the interviewer invites the narrator
to preserve historical content in folkloric form (Allen 1988, 21). The
interviewer is looking for the narrator to relate personal knowledge
to a past event. Alessandro Portelli takes this further when he says,

"Oral history shifts between performance-oriented narrative and
content-oriented document, between subject-oriented life story and
theme-oriented testimony. In practice, oral history stays mostly in

between: its role is precisely to connect life to times, uniqueness to representativeness, as well as orality to writing" (1997, 6).

For those of us who are caretakers of tape collections, we must never forget that stories are constructed, are recalled, and are retold because of a need and opportunity to convey meaning to others. Barbara Allen Bogart also reminds us that the process of creating narrative from experience is ongoing and perpetual; we do it all the time to suit our particular needs (Allen 1988). It is what makes the personal narative important. This is also why we speak not just of a story but of different tellings of a story. It is also why we must pay such close attention to the context and intended meaning of each telling. In this light, stories are a creative tool of expression as well as a body of knowledge, and as such they must be treated with deference to their fluidity.

And so, as I have pondered an interview with Ernest about the move to the new site and his boyhood recollections of that time, I have realized ever more clearly that the new telling will be carved out of a different rock, a different setting; it will be a different creation than the one I experienced back in 1997. Chances are, it will also be a commentary on the present.

Imagine, then, my surprise when I wrote to Ernest asking permission to use his story. He had a few corrections to make and I have made them, but he also had some startling updates. He reported that a casino has been built near the mountain and it is called Meropa, which means "drums." There are negotiations underway that may lead to a reclaiming of the site, but the place has changed a great deal, "almost beyond recognition." Ernest is unsure about the future of his boyhood home.

Tishu Ulen on a return trip to Wiseman. Photo by
Roger Kaye.

Gathering to Tell Stories
The Neglected Genre of Oral History

A small gathering of folks took time during the hustle and bustle of their holiday season to come to the public library to hear each other reminisce about Christmases past. Like many of the speakers who followed him, Jack's story was not only a window into the past but also a statement about what he thinks is valuable.

Jack grew up in Nenana, the son of storekeepers. He knew many of the folks that came to Nenana for supplies, to socialize, or to travel on the train. Many of them were bachelors who had come north, some to search for gold, others to trap; a few were dog team mail carriers. Nenana was the railroad and steamboat hub for the Interior. In summer and winter, freight and passengers came north on the train from Seward (an ice-free port). From Nenana, steamboats supplied the Tanana, Yukon, and Koyukuk Rivers during the summer months. In winter, overland trails connected the communities on the rivers to Nenana.

As Jack tells it, the bachelors looked forward to the holidays. One of the things they liked to do was order presents for kids. They'd place their order for a present, specifying for a girl or boy. They'd also chip in to order lots of nuts and candy to fill the kids' stockings. St. Mark's Episcopal mission and boarding school was in Nenana, so there were lots of kids in town. Jack recalls that on Christmas Eve the kids put on a skit for the community. Then, on Christmas Day, after church, there was a big meal for everyone in town. The way Jack recalls it, the festivities meant a lot to those old bachelors, who came to join in on the fun and help the kids have a good holiday. Jack concluded his story by saying that the value in the events was that "everyone knew and cared" (summary of remarks by Jack Coghill, Fairbanks, December 7, 1995).

In the past twenty-five years, Alaskans have shown interest in public forums and hearings. They have used them as a way to reminisce about the past, remind others of the good life, shape a sense of place, and comment on current issues of importance, like subsistence, land claims, and oil development. The hearing process has been used to testify for or against proposed legislation, review past legislative action, and seek redress. In all cases, the speakers have wanted the audience to know what they stand for and value.

All of these meetings have in common a public format where individuals can use stories to convey meaning to a large group. In hearings, it is assumed that testimony, based on personal experiences and oral tradition, will influence important decisions. Because of the setting and high expectations, there is often a strong emphasis on performance; speakers are seated at a microphone or literally on stage. If there are questions, they are usually posed at the end of an individual's testimony and meant to clarify, not engage the speaker in discussion. The setting differs from interviews, where the interviewer is a prominent and significant part of the record. Sometimes speakers at public forums are addressing outsiders who have influence over an issue under discussion. In other cases, such as the gathering where Jack told his Christmas story, the speakers just want to share what they remember with each other.

More than any other form of oral record, such hearings, forums, and storytelling sessions are Public, with a capital P. They are planned and announced. This genre focuses our attention on the reasons why people come forward specifically to tell stories, on how they shape the sessions, and on how they account for what previous speakers have said. For example, Jack was followed by Howard Luke and Robert Charlie; Howard confirmed Jack's story, and Robert extended the audience's sense of Christmas past to his boyhood in Old Minto. Some of these events produce a large volume of recordings, and often there is some form of publication. They receive a great deal of media attention when they take place, but this record is rarely consulted or referenced afterwards.

I am sure the speakers feel a sense of satisfaction that the stories have been recorded and hope their comments will be remembered, but the main emphasis is on the moment, the performance. Hence, I call this the neglected genre of oral narrative. The event attracts an audience, leaves a large record, but quickly fades from memory. On first glance, that seems like a big loss.

While most recorded testimonies are recent and rarely quoted, the genre is not new to Alaska. There is one famous hearing that produced a record that is often quoted. Back in 1915, when the gold mining activity in the Tanana Valley was shifting from pick and shovel to mechanized and large scale and the railroad was on its way, Alaska delegate to Washington James Wickersham convened a meeting of the Indian chiefs from the Tanana Valley. There was Chief Alexander of Tolovana; Julius Pilot, Chief Thomas from Nenana; Chief Ivan from Coskaket; Chief Charlie from Minto; Chief John from Chena; Chief Joe of Salchaket; Titus Alexander of Tolovana; and Alexander Williams, Jacob Starr, Johnny Folger, and Paul Williams of Fort Gibbon. The idea for the meeting developed after Wickersham met Chief Alexander out on the Tolovana River. Concerned about impending impacts on the Indians' way of life, Wickersham and Alexander planned a meeting to be held in Fairbanks that became known as the first Tanana Chiefs Conference (Wickersham Diary; Patty 1971; Mitchell 1997, 176–78).

At the meeting, the chiefs voiced strong opposition to reservations and, in elegant language, explained the importance of unrestricted access to the land and the game that was their livelihood. Chief Thomas from Nenana and Wood River told the assembled Indians and White officials: ". . . I am going to suggest one point, and that is that all of us Alaska Natives and other Indians will agree with us, that we don't want to be put on a reservation. You people of the Government, Delegate Wickersham, Mr. Riggs, and Mr. Richie, you people don't go around enough to learn the way that the Indians are living so we want to talk to you to explain our living to you, for we are anxious to show your people" (Patty 1971, 8).

This was one of the first times there was public recognition of conflicts between the two very different ways of looking at the land and the resources—between the Native dependance on customary land use and law for resolving resource access issues and the European, or Western, system of written and codified law, a system of land ownership with provisions for individual ownership, rights of acquisition, sale, and exclusion.

Why does this particular meeting last in people's minds, and why is it so often referenced and quoted while others have faded from conversation and even academic reference? To the best of my knowledge, this was the first gathering of the chiefs in the new town of Fairbanks. There were photographs taken. Participants included a prominent churchman, an official of the railroad (Alaska Engineering Commission), an agent of the General Land Office, and Wickersham, a man of prominence in Alaska and Washington. There was a recorder who made a written transcript of what the speakers said, and there was a newspaper article that appeared after the event (*Fairbanks Daily News-Miner*, 7 July 1915, p. 3). Wickersham's prominent role assured the event's place in academic history. Most significant, though, was the resurrection of the meeting's record from the Wickersham papers by journalist Stanton Patty. His republication of the transcript in a popular magazine at the time of the Alaska Native Land Claims (1971) demonstrated that the claims and concerns of the Natives were not new. The meeting is now viewed both as a benchmark of discussions between the government and Alaska Natives and as an example of the conflicts between the two ways of living in that place. Conflicting visions of land and resources continue to divide Alaskans and create dissension. But does this meeting deserve such prominent status? There is an earlier meeting that may be a more appropriate benchmark.

Seventeen years before the Tanana Chiefs gathering in Fairbanks, there was a meeting in Juneau of prominent local chiefs. It was called the Juneau School House Meeting (Hinckley 1970, 265–90), and it brought Southeastern Tlingit chiefs together to discuss the intrusion of miners on salmon streams owned by the Natives. Governor of the Territory of Alaska John Green Brady attended the meeting and spoke to the chiefs. The underlying themes there were analogous to those at the Tanana chiefs meeting—Native versus Western law—yet the Juneau meeting has been all but forgotten, except in the writing of historian Ted Hinckley and in reference by librarian and archivist Ronald Lautaret (1989, 46–47). I don't know why this is the case except that Hinckley's publication is fairly obscure and geared to the professional historian and, second, Wickersham had a prominent role at the Tanana Chiefs meeting. While Brady was an important figure in Alaska history, he has received little attention compared to Wickersham. Wickersham's presence at the Tanana Chiefs meeting assured a formal record, publicity, and later review by academics.

Both records fade from memory, but one much slower than the other, slower because there are continual reminders. The Tanana Chiefs Conference is the name adopted by Interior Athabascans for their Health and Social Service organization, and this perpetuates the name, as do periodic retellings and references to the first chief's meeting. Both Patty and Hinckley knew that the time was right to remember and retell, but Patty had a prominent public figure in Wickersham and a striking picture of the participants, and he chose a more popular venue to retell the story.

When Patty resurrected and republished the Wickersham record, there was public recognition of the need to address Native land issues, although there were probably few who knew the history of conflicts over land. The encroachment on Native land came to a head when the oil discoveries at Prudhoe Bay in 1968 precipitated a settlement that would permit development and a pipeline from the North Slope to tidewater (Berry 1975). Out of this came the Alaska Native Claims Settlement Act (ANCSA) in 1971 and later the Alaska National Interest Lands Conservation Act (ANILCA) in 1981.[17] These two acts precipitated a series of important hearings that formed baselines of public sentiment concerning ownership and management of public lands. In the early 1970s, the Joint Federal and State Land Use Planning Commission instituted meetings in many villages across the state. The purpose was to gather input from villagers on the federal land plans for the "D-2," or national interest, lands. These were extensive land tracts set aside under ANCSA whose future was to be determined under ANILCA. Some of the village hearings were recorded and archived.

The hearing in Beaver wasn't recorded, but as I recall, the challenge for the commissioners was to explain the full impact of the proposals and the changes that would be forthcoming in the management of land. The goal for villagers was to present their perspectives on how the proposals would change their way of life. Both communication tasks were daunting and precipitated lots of confusion and misunderstanding. This was the occasion when Moses Cruikshank rose to tell about his pick-and-shovel prospecting days. The hearings were extremely important because they represented one of the few opportunities the villagers had to be heard during the planning process. Despite their potential, I don't think the hearings made much difference in terms of shaping the proposals to Congress, and even though they are an important base to compare to the Alaska Native Review Commission Hearings held twenty years later, they are rarely consulted. In fact the recordings are slowly deteriorating, in part because they are not used.

Twenty years after passage of the Alaska Native Claims Settlement Act, the Alaska Native Review Commission hearings were held. They were designed to give communities a chance to evaluate the impact of land claims on their lives and make recommendations for legislative changes. The collected record has proved to be of some interest to students from rural Alaska, who can find recordings of elders from their home region. The elders give their perspectives on contemporary issues, topics familiar to the students and under consideration in their university classes. For the scholar, this record is a gold mine, a way to evaluate how issues have changed since the earlier hearings. Unfortunately, it is rarely used in this way, despite the fact that there are full transcripts, good access, and decent preservation.[18]

Elders conferences have become a popular format in Alaska to share traditional Native knowledge. Unlike the sessions mentioned so far, these have been locally controlled. The specifics differ by region, but the overall purpose is always to bring elders together so they can share their knowledge. The term *elder* is a bit elusive. It refers to older Native people whose experience, knowledge, and conduct is valued by their communities. In the early years, twenty years ago, the conferences didn't have focused topics, and elders would choose anything they wanted to share. In recent years, specific topics like medicine, child rearing, and subsistence issues have been emphasized. Most of these sessions have been recorded, but the existing record is small and scattered. The North Slope is a notable exception, because there was support for preservation and publication. Even there, publication has lagged far behind performance.

More could certainly have been done with the elders conferences to preserve and perpetuate the sharing of information, but that would have involved a different type of effort—archiving and publishing. I think it is fair to say that most of the groups who have undertaken these extra efforts have found them expensive and time consuming, and that it is very difficult to keep up an active archival and publication record as well as organize and conduct yearly conferences. When choosing between funding elders to come together and archiving and publishing, the former is seen as critical and the latter as nice when time and money permit. I think this is also the attitude of funding sources. It is easier to get money for a gathering than to fund publication of the results.

We can lament the lost opportunity to create a fuller record, but another way to look at this is to see the elders conferences first and foremost as performance settings, as events more than record, as tellings more than recordings, as an active process to create new settings for storytelling. In some cases, the old settings for storytelling don't exist anymore, and these new venues represent not so much a break from tradition as a recognition of a continuing need for such settings. The *qasgiq*, or men's house, was a gathering place for Eskimo people, a place where the old stories were told, including vital information on how to build and how to hunt and fish. Surrounded by skin boats or snowshoes under construction, a young person would be told the old stories, and the lessons of the past would be reinforced. Similarly, in the Interior, the Kk'adonts'idnee stories were told in the late fall and winter evenings in darkness or in dim light from candles or lantern, and they were a customary part of life to, as they say, "chew off part of the winter" (Nelson 1983, 1–2). These settings are gone, but the elders conferences with their formal structure and schedules carve out a new place for elders to teach, to share with each other, and to provide a link to the past. Somehow in our minds it is hard to appreciate that the new settings are just as important as the old and that the ways people create and respond to new settings deserve our attention.

This is certainly the case with the Communities of Memory project, which created local forums for community members to tell about their villages, towns, and cities. Like the elders conferences, these sessions were created for a specific purpose: both to reflect and shape people's sense of community. Unlike many of the above-mentioned hearings, the purpose was not to rectify, evaluate a condition, or preserve endangered knowledge, although it was hoped that the sessions would have a positive impact on how people see their community and the people who live there.

The sessions provided a new forum for people to come together to tell stories and to hear their neighbors' stories. The accounts ranged from "how I came to Juneau and fell in love with the country" to "in the good old days we really knew how to enjoy this place." Other themes emphasized the humor of a place, the racial prejudice, the outstanding characters, the lessons learned, and the great moments in the place's history—the kind of story Jack Coghill told at the Communities of Memory session in December 1995.

The project focused on ten communities, and a local committee made the arrangements and structured the sessions. People came out to share their sense of the place, to hear each other, and to help each other recognize and describe the community. The sessions demonstrated how people create a sense of place through stories. Phyllis Morrow has been closely involved with the project, and she describes the role of stories by saying, "Community is built as people have experience together, but also as they recollect their experiences."[19] As I review this record and talk with others who participated, it seems more and more clear that the emphasis was not so much on passing on knowledge as on using one's experiences and the storytelling session to add perspective to the present, to what's important today.

Nowhere was this more evident to me than in the Nome session I attended (chapter 3 above and Schneider 1998c). I heard three rather distinct groups of people—pioneers, new arrivals, and Natives—use stories in different ways to describe their sense of the place. The pioneers told about their ancestors and how they carved out a way of life in Nome, about the ties to the outside world, and about gold mining. For instance, Bunny Doyle Heiner opened her story by saying, "When I was a child growing up in Nome, I always was reminded of the Old Testament verse that said, 'there were giants in the world in those days.' The people that I knew when I was a kid in Nome seemed to me so much larger than life" (Sabo 1997, 112).

The newcomers used humor to tell about the fun they had in getting to know the community and about the wealth of opportunity to do new things. Howard Farley told about Joe Reddington Sr. and how the Iditarod sled dog race got started: "He knew it was possible. And you know, reading back into history, I knew it was possible. But boy, when we started this there were very few other people that believed this was possible, and they didn't believe we could run a second one, or a third one. And you want to remember, this race coming up this year will be the twenty-fourth annual Iditarod race" (Sabo 1997, 72).

The Natives told about the wisdom they had gained from parents and how important this traditional knowledge is, even today. Vernon Kugzruk told us, "I am very thankful for having been taught in that one particular era, where small children, eight, nine, ten years old were still taken out to learn some of the survival skills passed on to our parents from their parents as well" (Communities of Memory, Feb. 17, 1996).

Of course these are generalizations, but I think they give a picture, albeit grainy, of how people can use stories in a formal setting to project how they see themselves, their community, and how they want others to see and appreciate them. Afterwards, I learned that this was one of the first times that all three groups got together to tell their stories (Nancy Mendenhall, personal communication).

The Nome Communities of Memory project gave people in that place a chance to see themselves actively shaping various senses of their place, but I think articulation of that theme was less important to them than the act of telling their stories. Telling was more important than talking about the meaning of what was said. To be sure there were plenty of statements like, "as was said by . . ." or "let me add something about that." However, I think we have to separate the academic who finds the session a unique window into the people and their sense of place from the folks who tell the stories. The storytellers described how they see things and were less reflective about the differences between their experiences and descriptions. In all cases, there was a deep appreciation for a story well told and participants were left wondering what the impact had been of hearing each other's stories.

The Nome Communities of Memory project helped me come to the conclusion that I needed to consider at least four variables to really understand this session: (1) the setting and the audience; (2) the events that precipitated the narratives; (3) the influence of each speaker on the others; and (4) how individuals and groups used the setting to promote or build a point of view.

A few days after returning from South Africa in 1998, I delivered a paper on the Nome Communities of Memory session, and I couldn't help but compare the two settings: Nome, where there are the three active storytelling traditions and few signs of urgency to use story as a way to facilitate understanding across traditions, and South Africa, a country with many traditions, some shared, some quite separate, but a place that has chosen to use public storytelling to facilitate understanding at a national level. None of the Alaska sessions discussed here has had anywhere near the impact (scale, publicity, impact on participants) that the Truth and Reconciliation Commission's hearings have had in South Africa. The new government has aroused widespread interest in an examination of the past as it relates to apartheid, as a way to plan for the future, redress wrongs, and heal. The hearing process is one way they hope to accomplish this.

I heard about these hearings early on, and I followed newspaper reports. It was rare not to hear something about the commission in the news. There is even a World Wide Web Internet site for information (www.truth.org.za) and, while the sessions were in progress, a weekly television program reported key happenings of the past week. The hearings featured witnesses to and, in some cases, participants in the atrocities of the apartheid era, telling about that period of the nation's history.

The hope of the commission's leader, Archbishop Desmond Tutu, is that the retelling of the stories will give the nation a chance to come to understand, to reconcile through knowledge, and to move beyond the apartheid era into a new future. Perhaps this can be one case where the recognition of ubuntu is accepted and adopted by all (see chapter 4 above) For victims, the hearings are an opportunity to express what happened and publicly seek information about loved ones, and there is the possibility that they may be compensated in some way for what they have gone through.

For those accused of perpetrating crime, the hearings are a chance to explain their position, their actions, and their orders. The chance for amnesty is a strong incentive for them to come forward. While reparation or amnesty may be forthcoming, there are no guarantees (Perlman 1997, 6; Lyster 1997, 11).

The media plays a big part in reporting the Truth and Reconciliation hearings, and there is good reason for such attention. We need to hear the stories and work through the issues, but there are also inherent dangers in how the information is presented and represented. When I first arrived, I was fascinated by the Sunday night TRC Reports on television. They provided a visual and oral entrée into the hearing process. In time, I became disturbed by the use of dramatic music and the strongly moralistic role the moderator took in presenting the testimony. The reporting lacked balance, not in the facts, but in the way they were presented. The reporting was, in my estimation, sensational, inflammatory, and therefore dangerous.

The programs seemed to digest the information for the listener/viewer and left little room for alternate interpretations. I think it is fair to say that television is the way most people learn about the commission's work, and so reporting and retelling there are particularly important and should be subject to the highest degree of care. For scholars and the interested public, access to recordings of the hearings is still not universally available, so one is left for the time being with the media coverage. What seems to be needed is a format for analysis and review from multiple perspectives—a check and balance system.

This is a big and critical test for South Africans, with ramifications in other places where similar approaches are contemplated. The international community watches with great interest to see what the impact of the hearings will be. Perhaps the hearing process will have application to other parts of the world where there is similar strife, places like Rwanda and Serbia. As the horrors of the past are brought forward, there are those who feel relieved and ready to forgive and others who become hardened in their resentment toward perpetrators and the atrocities.

While the Truth and Reconciliation hearings have drawn international attention, there are other hearings going on in South Africa that will have impact on how the new democracy develops. One of these concerns the role of tribal chiefs and traditional leadership. How should the government create a role for the chiefs, and (a more basic question) who are the rightful chiefs and what counts in determining rights to power? A commission was formed to study the role of traditional leadership.[20]

The one hearing I attended focused not so much on how a chief's leadership is defined as on who was the rightful heir to a particular chiefdom, a real-life struggle recorded in front of the commission. Two leaders challenged each other's right to leadership. At the time, I concluded that the commissioners felt that they had to deal with specific cases in order to get at the dynamics of how traditional leadership works, as a first step toward drawing larger conclusions about the formal role the chiefs could play. I realized later that this type of struggle over rightful heirs to a throne is quite typical, and the use of historical reconstruction to test a candidate's authority is the way it is resolved. Considerable time and energy goes into these questions. This was true before apartheid; during apartheid, when the government manipulated the role of chief; and now after apartheid, with a commission that is trying to determine what role chiefs will have in the new government. In this light, it seems quite natural that the course of deliberations would follow traditional lines, and an understanding of this commission and how it functions must take into consideration this deeply ingrained African way of negotiating conflict.

The process of using a public forum to negotiate and promote a point of view is not unusual and should be a reminder that hearings are performances as much as records. Performance is shaped both by tradition and the perceived opportunity of the moment. For the participants, leaving a record is less important than convincing those in attendance.

Conclusion

We began by saying that public meetings are a neglected genre because they produce valuable records that are rarely referenced, gold mines waiting to be found. That still holds true, but we have also seen that they are performances in which the tellers are focused on the moment, what they want the audience to know then. When we think of the sessions in these terms, they provide a lively opportunity to observe how people interpret tradition, create order in their world, and attempt to shape the future. There is no better illustration of this than Job Kokachurak's story about the weather (retold in chapter 3). He chose the Communities of Memory session to speak about a current event, hunters stranded out in severe weather conditions. He shared the ancestors' knowledge about how to predict weather and told everyone to take heed.

This genre of storytelling poses special challenges to the curator of collections. First the curator must consider the event and how the participants shaped it to create meaning, then there is the physical record to be preserved, and finally there is the interpretation and representation of the record in the future. As we saw with the first Tanana Chiefs Conference, when the record is brought into focus to address a present concern, it gains new life. It is both reconsidered in its original light and in the new light of the present. Without such a comparative frame the accounts become frozen in time and revert to words rather than meaning.

These considerations are, of course, true for other types of stories that end up in the oral record, but the distinctiveness of this genre lies in the combination of the interaction of speakers and audience, the lack of an interviewer controlling the discussion, and the speaker's immediate focus on a primary audience of people present at an occasion rather than on some future listener.

The Tanana Chiefs. This is a famous image that has helped to preserve memory of the historic meeting of the chiefs. Photo 73-66-22N from the Vertical File, Individuals/Groups, Alaska and Polar Regions Archives, Rasmuson Library, University of Alaska Fairbanks.

Alfred Starr is seated on the right at the Alaska Native Review Commission Hearings. Alaska Native Review Commission Collection, Alaska and Polar Regions Archives, Rasmuson Library, University of Alaska Fairbanks.

Seven

In Search of the Story
Interviewers and Their Narrators

This chapter describes two projects where interviewers and their interviewees took their discussion to a larger audience in very different ways and a third project that is ripe with potential for description and interpretation. In all three, multiple perspectives on a theme form the basis to understand and appreciate, in the first case, the experiences of Native artists and their communities, in the second, the Native history of the Yukon coastline, and in the last case, the history of a university in South Africa where the struggle against apartheid was dramatically played out.

The Artists behind the Work

The Artists behind the Work project grew out of discussions between Terry Dickey and Wanda Chin of the University of Alaska Museum; Suzi Jones, formerly of the Alaska State Council on the Arts; and myself. Terry is an anthropologist and specializes in museum design and educational outreach; Wanda is an exhibit designer. She and Terry designed the exhibit and the catalog for *The Artists behind the Work*. Suzi Jones is a folklorist and was working extensively with Native art in her position as director of the Traditional Native Arts Program. We designed a project that combined biographies of four Native artists, a traveling museum exhibit, and a publication that featured the artists and their work. The theme reinforced in the exhibit and the catalog was the role art plays in Native communities and in the lives of the artists.

From the start, we knew that Native art has a social, ceremonial, and utilitarian role that is different from Western art, which is often oriented exclusively toward display and/or adornment. (There are of course interesting exceptions such as the quilts discussed in chapter 3.)

The project featured interviews with Nick Charles Sr., from the Yup'ik region of Southwest Alaska; Frances Demientieff, an Athabascan from Interior Alaska; Lena Sours, an Inupiaq from Northwest Alaska; and Jennie Thlunaut, a Tlingit from Southeast Alaska. One of the distinguishing features of Native artists is the diversity of things they do; it's inappropriate to define their work too narrowly. With that as a caution, but for the purposes of this discussion, we will say that Nick is especially recognized for his masks, Frances for her beadwork, Lena for her skin sewing, and Jennie for her Chilkat blankets.

Four very talented and well-connected researchers wrote their biographies: Ann Fienup-Riordan did the interviews and wrote the essay on Nick. At that time, Ann was already a recognized expert on Yup'ik culture and had worked on Nelson Island, where Nick was from, and at Bethel, where Nick was living at the time of the project. Katherine McNamara, an accomplished writer, worked with Frances Demientieff and was assisted by family members like her good friend Martha Demientieff. Sharon Moore and Sophie Johnson are from Kotzebue, where Lena Sours lived. Sharon and Sophie received help from other community members such as Rachel Craig, who is a recognized expert on Inupiaq culture. Rosita Worl and Charles Smythe researched and wrote the essay on Jennie Thlunaut. Rosita was particularly qualified for the research because of her background in anthropological research, because she is Tlingit from Klukwan, and because Jennie is her grandmother. The close ties of these researchers to the featured artists provided the basis for in-depth work and a sense of common commitment by interviewers and narrators. This was not the all-too-familiar scenario in oral history of "outsiders" who come in to interview.

As the artists and other community members described how they learned their craft, we could see how Native art is an integral part of the social, ceremonial, and subsistence life of the artist and his or her community.

Nick Charles, Yup'ik Mask Maker

Nick Charles's story has held a powerful message for me because I am trying to learn how to work with wood, and Nick's account reminds me of how long it takes to really become good at it. Nick described to Ann Riordan how he grew up in the *qasgiq* (men's house), where he was introduced to the art of carving. The young boy began with the shavings on the floor—their even, smooth shape was the work of master carvers: "Men lived in a world carpeted with wood chips. In fact, the quality and quantity of the shavings surrounding each man's place in the qasgiq were a visible mark of his energy and skill" (Riordan 1986, 32).

When Nick grew older, he learned how to select driftwood for carving, learned to carve net floats and paddles, and only after many years of practice began to carve masks for community dances. Part of the reason for this was that mask dancing was forbidden for a long time, but the point that impresses me is that the skills needed to do such carving took many years to perfect. Not all men carved well enough to produce the intricate masks, but all men had to carve the basic items like paddles and net floats since they were a necessary part of making a living. Today, these men know and appreciate good carving and have a sense for what it takes to produce the masks (Riordan 1986, 29–57).

In a series of interviews, Nick introduced Ann to the intricacies of what it takes to be a good carver, but Ann also brought an important perspective to the dialogue, her interest in Yup'ik world view and cosmology. She spent years learning about this part of Yup'ik life, and that gave her a basis to ask about and pursue that aspect of mask making. This took the discussion beyond techniques of carving and even beyond the stories told by the masks and the dancers to the ceremonial and spiritual life represented in the way the masks are constructed. For instance, at a mask-making workshop, Nick carved a mask depicting the shaman's vision of the first White men who would come, a representation of the traditional story of Issiisasaayuq's vision. Nick described the mask he carved: "The mask is the eye of the dance." Ann interprets: "It is the vision of this vision that he set out to capture in wood" (Riordan 1986, 48). Ann explains that the dance, the mask, and the story are part of a whole that includes representation of history (the story of the first Whites), prophesy (the prediction that Whites would come), and Yup'ik cosmology (the eyes representing passages into other forms and worlds, and by extension, visions and transformations) (Riordan 1986, 46–49). The integration of form, function, and belief follows tradition but leaves room for the artist/storyteller/dancer to be creative. This information was not common knowledge; without the specialized background, knowledge, and interests of both Nick and Ann this record would not be available, and it is a tribute to both that they were able to document and describe this important part of Yup'ik life.

Jennie Thlunaut, Chilkat Blanket Maker

Jennie Thlunaut was one of the last people to know how to make Chilkat blankets, and her story describes this work. Going beyond that, Rosita and Chuck provide examples from their interviews of the social and ceremonial use of art in Tlingit culture. This is illustrated in a story of the Chilkat shirt Jennie made for Jimmie Marks, a man who had formally adopted her as a sister:

> When Jimmie Marks became ill, Jennie was so worried that she would not have any money to give in his honor when he died. She recalls the distress she felt. "What we [I] going to do when he died. I got nothing . . . I got no money." At that point, she decided to make him a Chilkat shirt. When she finished the shirt she went down to Juneau to visit him. He had recently been released from the hospital. She approached him, "I just came to see you. I worry about [you]. I thinking about you all the time. I got no brother, that's why I'm glad you adopt me for your sister . . . What we going to do when you go away? That's why I make something for you." (Worl and Smythe 1986, 141)

As Rosita points out, the shirt became more than a gift and a representation of a social bond; it became a representation of the Tlingit values of respect, obligation, and reciprocity. Jennie showed respect for the honor Jimmie bestowed on her; she was obligated to reciprocate, and she found a way to do it that would have meaning for many generations to come. The story will continue to be told as the shirt is worn at special times by future generations of Chilkat Tlingit (Worl and Smythe 1986, 127–46). Rosita was uniquely qualified to retell this story because she grew up familiar with Tlingit protocol and values, the aspects of Jennie's work that she interprets and describes so well from the interviews.

Frances Demientieff, Bead Worker

Katherine McNamara's interviews with Frances Demientieff provide examples of how art reflects its integration into the social and aesthetic life of the community: "As a young wife, Frances learned what other wives learned, that is to do fancy work for their husbands. Women were taught not to brag about their accomplishments, but when they sent husbands and sons off to Sunday Mass in fancy work hats and gloves . . . they were able to show off their work without having to draw unwelcome attention to themselves. Yet everyone could see their talents and their social status was thus enhanced" (McNamara 1986, 87).

Katherine and Frances also talked about how women made their designs and how the designs are identified with individuals and the region. The choice of beads, colors, patterns, and techniques reflect the delicate balance between the structure imposed by cultural standards of how the work is to be done and, where there is room, the individual creativity by the artist.

In a very subtle way, Frances's choice of colors and flowers reflect the local environment.

"You watch the flowers as they grow and try to copy them" (1986, 90). Martha Demientieff told Katherine that "This is a complex identity. Yet each woman owns her own patterns and works her own colors and combinations of colors . . . We value our personal freedom: no one can tell anyone else what to do. Yet we can only be individuals within the group" (1986, 88).

The Artists behind the Work project was successful because the topic is of wide interest to people, the insights into Native art expanded understanding among all of us, and the story was retold well in the catalog and the traveling exhibit. None of this would have been possible without the contributions of the museum staff and the interviewers and narrators, who worked well together to explore dimensions of the theme. The project exemplifies the importance of (1) a good project theme, (2) knowledgeable narrators and interviewers who work well to explore aspects of the theme, and (3) effective formats (like a traveling exhibit and pretty catalog) and skilled exhibit designers for retelling the story to future audiences. Moreover, community members saw the project as important and supported it.

Yukon North Slope Inuvialuit Oral History

You can't spend much time learning about commercial whaling in the Arctic without hearing about Herschel Island and the ships that overwintered there. That story has been eloquently told (see Bockstoce 1995), but the accounts of the Inuit and Inupiat people who lived at Herschel were stories still waiting to be told. It was logical for the Yukon and federal governments to fund a project to document the history of Inuit use of the island, and for the Inuvialuit to design and run it.

Soon after the interviews began, the project director, Murielle Nagy, realized that it was best to consider Herschel Island within the context of many other places connected with subsistence activities, employment opportunities, and governmental and religious institutions. She realized that a narrow, site-specific focus was a Western, not an Inuit, way of looking at the place (Nagy 1994, xi; see also Nagy 1991a and b). Therefore, she expanded the scope of the project to reflect historical and cultural reality.

I was invited as an advisor on the 1990 expedition. We did some interviewing in Aklavik and then traveled by small boat across the delta to Shingle Point, where we camped for several days before heading farther west along the coast and finally out to Herschel Island. As we traveled and camped, the elders told stories about the places, about how they migrated to the Yukon, and about other topics such as Indian-Eskimo relations, schooling, shamans, and how they made a living on the coast and inland. We came to appreciate a gradual shift in focus and residence from the west, Herschel Island, to the east, the Mackenzie Delta, as economic and government services provided new opportunities and as resources became scarce on the coast. Although there are written sources that can confirm this narrative, it is worth retelling from the Inuvialuit stories because they illustrate how they see their personal history.

The Uummarmiutum, or Nunatarmiut, are the principal group of Inuvialuit who live on the Yukon coastline. They migrated from Alaska, starting in the 1870s, when the caribou declined in Northwest Alaska (Nagy 1994, 1). They were not the first people to live on the Yukon coastline (Nagy 1994, 29), but they became the predominant group. At the turn of the century, commercial whalers began wintering over at Herschel Island. Pauline Cove provided a safe and secure harbor for their ships. Peter Thrasher's father was from Alaska and moved to Herschel Island during the American whaling period. Peter told Murielle about the whalers: "There were lots of them. Sometimes they say that about thirty or forty ships were here, also whaling boats. There was lots of them. The big ship would go travel to Vancouver Island or B.C. or the states, you know? After they load up their ships with whale oil in them big barrels, the one they boil inside the ships. There was lots of them" (PT90-9A: 5, Nagy 1994, 33).

The Inuvialuit were attracted to the employment opportunities, particularly as meat hunters for the crews. Following the whalers came the Royal Canadian Mounted Police, trading posts, and the

Anglican Church. When commercial whaling declined, the mission was moved east to Shingle Point, in 1920 (Nagy 1994, 39). The Hudson's Bay Company had a trading post there, and by 1929, there was an Anglican school. The school continued until 1936 when it was moved to Aklavik (Nagy 1994, 44). By then, the Hudson's Bay Company had also moved from Shingle Point. Flooding and a scarcity of resources on the coast led many people to move to the delta.

When I returned from the 1990 trip, I had learned the broad outlines of this movement and had heard stories of the earlier migration from Alaska to the Yukon. But this wasn't something Murielle focused on exclusively. She let the interviews evolve, and she followed the Inuvialuit's lead. Now, as I review her publication, I am impressed by the skillful way she has presented this and other themes. There are two texts in her publication—her generalized introduction to a topic and quotations from the narrators who describe their experience or understanding of the subject. This approach differs from *The Artists behind the Work* project in that the narrators dictated the order and Murielle then used short introductions to contextualize their stories for the reading audience. In *The Artists behind the Work*, the narrators' quotes are used sparingly to illustrate. In the Inuvialuit oral histories, they drive the organization and writing. For instance, many of the interviews discuss the relation between Inuvialuit and the Gwich'in Athabascans from Old Crow. Murielle introduces the topic with a sidebar (which I will represent in italics), and then the Inuvialuit elders' quotes are presented. The following is an extract:

Inuvialuit and Indian Relations

The Inuvialuit, who occupied the Yukon coast and particularly the Nunatarmiut who had migrated through the Old Crow Flats from inland Alaska, developed a friendship with the Gwich'in of Old Crow. Dora Malegana relates the first time she met Indians:

"First time I saw Indians, it was really smelling smoke, really! You know that was Caroline Moses and her granddad. She started talking in Loucheaux (Gwich'in) to Annie Joe (Inglangasuk) and then she started looking at Jean. When I looked at Annie, she was talking in Loucheux really good like this." (1994, 108)

The Inuvialuit story of Indian-Inuit relations is multifaceted because some of them shared a great deal with the Old Crow Athabascans. They learned each other's language and dances, shared hunting territory, intermarried, and frequented the same trading posts. That's the general topic behind Dora Malegana's story, and it is interesting given the popularly held, although misleading, notion that Indians and Inuit did not like to interact. Beyond that generalization, though, and even more interesting are particular descriptions of the interaction, for that is where narrators' observation take us directly to experiences and what it was like to be there. Murielle recognized and understood how to create an outline to accommodate the things narrators stressed, and then she used Inuvialuit descriptions to present their understandings of the topics.[21]

The University of the North Oral History Project

The UNIN oral history project began in January 1997 in Sovenga, South Africa. From the start, the program was based on design by consensus. A committee was formed of university library staff members, who made all of the decisions—what themes to emphasize, who to interview first, and who should take the lead as interviewer in each session. Unlike the first two projects just described, in this one, most committee members attended the interviews. This could be overwhelming. I recall an interview with an Afrikaner history professor. It was held at my residence. I didn't pick up on it at the time, but my colleagues made note of how, since he was probably expecting to talk just with me, when he entered the room and saw all the library staff, it threw him off balance and made him ill at ease. That was certainly not our intent, but everyone was eager to be there and that's the way we proceeded.

Now that the project has produced a cache of important interviews, it is time to create products that will illustrate the experiences of the people who shaped and were shaped by the institution and to tell stories of how this place plays a part in the nation's history of resistance to apartheid.

One of the realities of oral history that we keep returning to is that we understand what someone says in an interview only when we can imagine what they are describing, and imagination depends upon experience. The interview with the history professor is an example. My colleagues found the session revealing because he appeared defensive and tried to paint a picture of himself as someone whose family had always worked for the common good of all Africans. The interviewers pointed out that he came from a predominantly Afrikaner part of the country that had a reputation for not supporting Black Africans. They questioned him hard about his interrogation of Es'kia Mphahlele and how he had dismissed this Black candidate for a position at the university because he had left the country during the apartheid struggle.[22]

My impressions of the interview differed slightly. I saw a man who was steeped in a rigid sense of order, was authoritarian, looked to his superiors for direction, and had chosen to focus on university management instead of historical research. I imagined that his interest in control was a vestige from earlier years when it was the norm for university administrators to rule with absolute authority. The exchange between interviewers and the professor over the hiring focused at one point on the fact that Mphahlele had left the country during the harshest years of apartheid, had written in a critical way about conditions, and wasn't present to constructively bring about change. The professor argued that he should have stayed in South Africa, that he had abandoned his country, so didn't deserve a position. The interviewers, on the other hand, saw him as a hero who had to leave to be effective in his work, and they believed that the system suppressed him. I could understand, although not excuse, the professor's self-centered approach. In his privileged position, he would not have felt the same stress the young candidate felt since life was probably good for him in the apartheid years. Unfortunately, and surprising to me, although not to my colleagues at UNIN Library, the professor's position was undoubtably shaped by his Afrikaner background and the values it promoted, although caution must be taken in generalizing about these influences.

The other interviewers were interested in the stance the professor took on the hiring and in how he could defend himself, and they saw his response as totally inadequate. I was less interested in judging his response or seeing it as a coverup. I wanted to know how he could have acquired such an attitude. Each approach is worth considering, but they reveal the differences in experiences between the other interviewers and myself. They had a justified suspicion of this man, whereas I knew him less well and had not been subject to his influence. Our differences open, rather than foreclose, future analyses of the record.

Professor E. Frederik Potgieter was the first rector of the University of the North, and many of the interviews described his background as an anthropologist and specialist in the Bantu languages. Given the government's philosophy of using ethnic distinctions to create separate homelands and segregated populations—to make separate settlements based on language and cultural traits—it was in keeping that a man with Potgeiter's qualifications would be chosen to head this university. He is remembered in the interviews as authoritarian, for his knowledge of languages, as someone who knew everything that was going on, and as a fearless lion hunter.

The interviews demonstrate that while he wasn't liked, he was respected. His tenure as rector preceded much of the public unrest that led to the overthrow of the system. So we don't know how he would have fared if he had remained as head in later times. And we don't know how perceptions of him have been influenced by the changes that occurred after he left office. The rectors who followed him were generally neither liked nor respected.

The evolution of leadership as recalled in the descriptions of the rectors is an important theme that could be developed from the interviews. There was interplay between the directors' personalities, the political climate during their tenure, and the evolution of national policies that officially marked their administrations. I suspect that such a multifaceted analysis could produce a picture that would be similar to people's perceptions of other sectors of life in the country in the years leading up to, during, and after the overthrow of apartheid.

All of the UNIN interviews were highly charged with politics but not all related to the government or even the university. One of the most interesting was with members of the leading faction of the Mamabola people, the tribal group who live where the university is located. Our goal was to have them describe their history of relations with the university, including the original transfer of land. The interview was steeped in protocol. First, as a group, we traveled to the court of the Mamabola, and after offering some money, we were given an audience with the chief and his court. A formal interview time was set up for a meeting at the university. They produced a formal written document that was presented and read into the record. Then, with the others present, several spokesmen gave their stories of the history. Then everyone retired to the dining room where there was a meal. The Mamabola were all elderly men and they dressed in suits and ties. This was the first time that they had been asked to come to the university, and they said they were pleased for the opportunity.

I was especially impressed by two things: first, the formality of the interview, including the fact that they provided a written statement, and second, that they came as a group—no one spoke alone. We were aware that there was a splinter group that also had claims and that our interview with the predominant faction would be subject to scrutiny and interpretation. We tried to avoid getting into the middle of their dispute, since that was not our interest, and we knew that if we weren't careful the interview might turn into a justification of their position of power vis-à-vis the other group. We chose not to interview the other faction because we thought we could get the information we needed from the primary group, and it was easier to avoid tribal politics by working with the group in power.

Perhaps the biggest challenge in any retelling of the UNIN story in publication or media is the tendency to generalize about and focus exclusively on the bad Afrikaners and the good Black people. This is precisely why the oral history is so important, because the narrators move beyond generalizations to their interpretation of how they proceeded in difficult times. This is evident in the case of Professor Manaka, the university librarian, who describes how he became the head librarian and the way he exerted his leadership, despite discrimination. His energy went into working through the system as opposed to striking out at it. This is echoed by Professor Mawasha, who describes how he arrived at UNIN straight from Johannesburg and looked around at the fields and farmers. He asked himself: why stay here? Then he thought of the life of poverty he left in the city, and despite the problems of UNIN, he recognized it as a place to get an education and escape the poverty back home.

Thoko Hlatywayo had a slightly different interpretation of what Professor Mawasha meant. She noted that he wasn't so much afraid of poverty back home but of arrest. She notes, "He could not go back for fear of being arrested for violating pass laws. The position was that if a Black male was found 'loitering' in town or in the location where he was staying, he would be arrested by the police and sent to jail" (Hlatywayo, personal communication).

Creating the Record

When most oral historians talk about oral history, they describe settings where an interviewer directs questions to narrators and together they create a meaningful record. Portelli puts it this way: "Oral history expresses the awareness of the historicity of personal experience and of the individual's role in the history of society and in public events" (1997, 6). The creative activity takes place at several levels: in project design and approach, in how the interviewer builds evidence for diverse perspectives, and in the narrator's knowledge and ability to express what he or she knows. A good interview adds new information about a topic and leads the listener into a fuller understanding of the event or person being discussed. Carrie Kline says, "Let's step back and envision the possibilities for producing a body of work that reflects a series of subjective truths, but combines these personal testimonies so as to create a multi-dimensional product—a story no one person could have told" (1996, 20). For this approach to work well, both interviewer and narrator must work together to create meaning. The process depends on the interview context, trust, knowledge of the subject, understanding each other's interests and backgrounds, and agreement on what directions the discussion should take.[23] In the final part of the creative process, the interviewer/writer/producer must convey the story to others. There is a shift from story shared with interviewer to story preserved for and presented to future audiences.

The three projects just discussed point to several things worthy of consideration. First, the interviewer and his or her background, experiences, interests, and relationships with other community members are critical to motivating narrators to share their knowledge and to understanding what is said. Second, a thematic approach allows you to gather a variety of perspectives on a topic, but the theme must be flexible, adaptable to the various ways community members choose to use it as a starting point for their narration. Themes are a springboard for elaboration, not a fence that delineates the bounds of discussion. The best oral history invites narrators to carve out personal perspectives, calls for interviewers to pick up on extensions, and invites elaboration.

Third, as demonstrated in examples one and two, the creative process does not end with a good interview; it continues through archiving, publication, and/or media production. Interviewers are called upon to highlight the themes, show the different perspectives, and lead the reader/listener/viewer into the experiences of the narrators. In recent years, the documentary filmmaker Ken Burns has very successfully employed interviews, historic photographs, and archival film footage to bring important stories to public attention. A key to the success of his approach is the diversity of perspectives provided by the people interviewed.

Interviewers and, by extension, archivists, who manage the record, are links to future audiences. Their retelling, just as their interviewing, is an art, a composition designed for future audiences. Nowhere is this more obvious than in life histories based on oral history. That's where we turn our attention next.

This is the cover to the University of Alaska Museum catalog for *The Artists behind the Work*. The project coordinator was Terry Dickey, the project designer was Wanda Chin, and the guest curator and editor was Suzi Jones. Featured on the cover, top to bottom, are Nick Charles, Lena Sours, Frances Demientieff, and Jennie Thlunaut.

Mamabola leaders at lunch after their interview at the University of the North. The photo was probably taken by Kgwerano Isaac (Ike) Matibhe.

This photo was taken for the Herschel Island Cultural Study by John Tousignant of the Yukon Heritage Branch. Left to right are Renie Arey, Murielle Nagy, Dora Malegana, Jean Tardiff, Kathleen Hansen, and Sarah Meyook. Photo courtesy of the Yukon Heritage Branch and the Inuvialuit Regional Corporation.

Life Histories
The Constructed Genre

South Africa, Sunday, June 8, 1997: Page two of the *Sunday Times* announces that Professor Charles Van Onselen's book *The Seed is Mine* was the winner of this year's Alan Paton award for nonfiction. The book captured my attention because it is so thoroughly researched and well written. It is the story of Kas Maine, a Black sharecropper whose life spanned the period 1894–1985. I say the book is well written because it paints a very vivid picture of this man's life and the struggle he faced to make ends meet. We see not only Maine's trials but also his skill and wisdom, his judgment, and his response to failure and success. His story is a grim reminder of the apartheid era and the lives of Black dry land farmers. The book is also of interest because it raises questions about the roles of writer and teller in life history.

Van Onselen would have us believe that his book reflects Maine's thinking and decision making, but it is more accurate to say that the book is Van Onselen's reconstruction—based on his knowledge of the history and of Maine's life and on what Maine said in interviews—of what he thinks Maine was thinking. Sixty-six interviews with Maine and 137 with his family and others, to say nothing of Van Onselen's other research, qualify him to speak with authority, but we must not be lulled into thinking that Maine is speaking. The book is written in third person, with the author speaking about Maine, not Maine speaking about his own life. Consider the following description of mechanization on the farm:

> Toward the end of 1942, the onslaught of Nazi U-boats on Allied shipping in the Atlantic reduced the supplies of agricultural machinery, equipment, spare parts, and fuel reaching South Africa to a trickle, and the pressure on the land occasioned by the expansion in mechanized production started to ease. By 1943 it was official government

policy to encourage white farmers "to make greater use of animal power," and thus the great global conflict, which at first had restricted hope for the Triangle's increasingly vulnerable black tenants, came to offer a respite.

Kas could hardly have chosen a more propitious moment to re-enter the world of "white" agriculture. Not only had he sat out the early years of the war as an artisan-cum-livestock speculator at Kareepoort but, at the age of forty-seven, he could call on the services of two wives and eight children at a time when agricultural producers were once again strongly reliant on manual labor. As physically strong as he was tall and lean, he was making good headway in his career as a farmer and believed he had the necessary experience, equipment and livestock to make a success of his new ventures. He knew that Goosen could be an awkward and demanding landlord, but he hoped their shared desire for material progress would overcome the difficulties in their relationship. If there was enough rain and the markets remained buoyant, he could compete with the best in the district: his arch-rival Johnson Xaba and the others in RaKapari's drinking circle would have to look to their laurels. (1996, 238–39)

As this quote illustrates, Van Onselen did his homework and knows a great deal about Kas Maine and the forces that operated on his life. What we don't get much of from this work is Kas's description of how things unfolded, how he saw the impact of mechanization, how he felt about opportunity. The book is obviously a valuable contribution to our knowledge of what a sharecropper's life was like, but as a biography, it represents one end of the spectrum of how such books can be written. It leads us to ask, what would Kas Maine's story be like in his own words? While there are quotes, I, for one, want to hear more of his voice, his thinking.

This is certainly Christopher Lee's evaluation, although he is more willing to accept the omission of the subject's voice than I am. Invoking the famous American story of Nate Shaw, a southern sharecropper, Lee excuses Van Onselen and the "Western biographical form":

What cognitive categories and perspectives are lost when an informant's voice is replaced by the historian's? Is it worthwhile to sacrifice the informant's idiosyncrasies for the purposes of narrative flow and Western understanding? Perhaps rather than comparing the book to *All God's Dangers* it is more apt to consider this book more generally as an example of the basic Western biographical form that carries no specific obligation to convey the subject's voice. (1999, 134)

There are two issues here and they are not distinct. First, there is the question of the narrator's voice and how he (Kas Maine) speaks about issues. That is my prime criticism of Van Onselen's work. We also have to consider the "authoring function," that is, the role of the writer/interviewer/compiler in determining the direction of the text and the editing he did for a new audience, the people who buy and read the work. As author, he assumes immense authority and power over Maine's story.

Van Onselen's wife, Belinda Bozzoli, and her co-researcher, Mmantho Nkotsoe, have written a book about women from Phoekeng, an area in northwest South Africa. They use life history to trace the experiences of the women, their time spent in Johannesburg doing domestic work, and their return to Phoekeng. The result is a social history of specific lives written to illustrate the experiences of many women from the region. The value of this approach is that by introducing many different voices Bozzoli and Nkotsoe are able to illustrate the variety of conditions their subjects faced and the responses over their lifetimes. In this respect, the book is instructive (Bozzoli 1991). The disadvantage is that we never seem to hear enough from each woman to get a sense of who she is and how she makes sense of her lifetime of experiences. Instead, the individual is highlighted as an example of a response to a situation, not as a person we come to know over the span of her life. Another drawback is that the predominant voice is that of the principal writer, who carefully guides the text and relegates the narrators' voices to the role of illustration. The narrators' accounts are valued for what they say, but little attention is given to the way the narrators construct their story. The book is about these women, not by them.

Consider Andor Skotnes's remarks at the 1995 meeting of the South African Society of Archivists:

> My belief is that the most rewarding approach to oral history is the life history approach. With its academic roots in the qualitative methodologies of sociology and anthropology, and its popular roots in traditional storytelling, the life history approach encourages informants to take the initiative in reconstructing their experiences; to speak freely, expansively, and to follow tangents; to explore the interrelationships of experiences over time; to examine the lived

"interior"—the subjective dimension—of the historical process. While life history interviews do not necessarily deal with the whole process of their informants' lives, they always strive to contextualize the experiences under consideration within the complexity of the informants' life processes. (1995, 66)

Skotnes's approach is more akin to what I call oral biography, that is, the story of a person's life told in their own words but compiled and edited for publication by a writer. The writer's role in this endeavor varies from one extreme, where he or she is a major voice, to the other, where the writer is barely noticeable. David Dunaway points out three variations on this theme: (1) those life histories that are informed by oral interviews but of which the interviews are only a part; (2) multiple interviews with different people who provide perspectives on the subject of the life history; and (3) what Dunaway refers to as the "oral memoir," which features the subject telling his or her own story, with the writer adding explanation and footnotes (1991, 257). Van Onselen's and Bozzoli's work are clearly of type one. In this chapter, we will concern ourselves with type three and the variations afforded in the "oral memoir," what I call "oral biography."[24]

At one extreme of type three, the oral biography, there are books like the series published by the Yukon-Koyukuk School District here in Alaska. These first appeared in the early 1980s, and they have been immensely popular in the villages. They feature individuals from each of the communities of the school district and contain a generous array of historical and recent photos. They are oblong in shape, in what I think of as coffee table style, with wide pages that easily stretch out on your lap for viewing when two or more people sit together.

The audience for the Yukon-Koyukuk oral biography series is primarily community members, and the books are commemorative in nature. The series was the idea of an innovative member of a rural school district and two very talented researchers and writers, Yvonne Yarber and Curt Madison. They traveled to the villages in the region and asked the communities to select elders to be featured. They worked with twenty-two regional elders and with Andrew Isaac, the traditional chief at the time, to produce the books that make up the series, a wonderful tribute to the featured elders and a rich resource on the region. Since the audience for the books is the local communities, the writer/compilers do not spend time recontextualizing for new audiences, and readers find themselves moving from one topic to another with little regard for chronology or even relationship of topic. One is left with a mosaic of information that becomes a generalized background for understanding the person featured and their experience.

Another book that follows this same approach is *Shandaa*, Belle Herbert's story, recorded by Bill Pfisterer and first published in 1982. The major effort in this work was to get Belle's story down. Belle was believed to be over 100 years old at the time. Her own experiences along with the stories she grew up with bridged most of the historical period. For instance, she talked about army officer Patrick Henry Ray, who traveled the Yukon at the height of the Gold Rush in 1897 and reported to Washington on conditions in the territory (1992, 126–27). We have his reports, but now to have her oral account adds local perspective on the man and his expedition. While Bill was the compiler, Belle really told her stories to her granddaughter, often addressing her directly.

> Yes, that's when they [horses] arrived.
> And they killed all those cows.
>
> That
> Captain Ray I'm talking about, he
> built that store
> and brought a lot of food with the
> steamboat;
> he was going to stay there and
> those people who were going to stay there
> all died.
> They were Outside people
> and they all died off . . .
>
> Ah grandchild!
> It was very poor at that time, and finally
> little by little the white people came.
>
> Even so
> there were not very many people but
> here and there, from time to time,
> they sometimes came around.
>
> That's
> the way it was.
> the white people just came gradually.
>
> (1982, 127)

For local audiences who know the elders, these biographies work quite well. This is because they can imagine the elder telling the story and because they have, as Chase Hensel says, "shared cultural assumptions."[25] The shared assumptions are gained from living similar lives, feeling similar things, and from a background of references to other tellings. But how well will these transfer to their children and to other audiences who don't know the elders featured? Certainly, any reader is left with an impression of the person and some of the events that influenced his or her life, but the further removed we are from the life and times of the elder, the more incomplete and incomprehensible the picture. The foreign and distant reader needs more background information.

Somewhere in the middle—between the biographies that hide the writer's voice and those where the narrator's voice is merely invoked to illustrate, there is a literature that seeks to both preserve voice and story and to provide ample context for future generations.

This is what we are trying to do in the Oral Biography Series at the University of Alaska Fairbanks. The series was started in 1986 when Moses Cruikshank's book, *The Life I've Been Living*, was published. The goal was to use oral history recordings to create the story of a person's life in their own words with minimal but adequate commentary by the compiler. This book was followed in 1991 by Waldo Bodfish's *Kusiq: an Eskimo Life History from the Arctic Coast*. These titles, along with Margaret Blackman's two books published by the University of Washington Press, *During My Time: Florence Edenshaw Davidson, a Haida Woman* and *Sadie Brower Neakok, an Inupiaq Woman*, helped define a friendly debate for Margay and me. We both agree that there is need to let tellers tell their story and also that writers are asked by their audiences (if they are more than very local and time bound groups) to provide context, further clarification, and explanation. The issue revolves around how to provide context without usurping the voice of the teller. Margay and I just can't agree on where the context stuff goes. I maintain that it should all be buried in the back after the teller tells his or her story, and Margay demonstrates in her work that you can have it up front without usurping the teller's voice. Her Davidson book has a whopping sixty-two pages of preparation before Florence tells her story, and yet we never fail to recognize and identify Florence's voice. Notice that both of us, in the spirit of Skotnes's quote, are concerned primarily about tellers and their stories, told their way and in their words.

We both see the challenge in how the narrator's story is represented in the written retelling. Our dilemma is how to translate to a broader audience the sharing that took place between the narrator and ourselves, to determine what is needed in the way of explanation, and then to figure out how to integrate it so that it supports and does not usurp the teller's voice. It is all about the art of retelling.

In the beginning of the Davidson book, Margay makes the point that biography is as much about the writer as about the teller.

> Finally, although some anthropologists, such as Kluckhohn (1945, 97), have regretted the intrusion of the anthropologist into the native life-history document, it goes without saying that the relationship between anthropologist and life-history subject is critical to the telling of the story in the first place and ultimately to the understanding of the final record. I agree with Brumble, who notes that much of the fascination [with life histories] is a result of, rather than in spite of their being so often collaborative. (Blackman 1982, 15)

If we ignore the role of the writer, we risk losing perspective on the relationship between the teller and the writer. We forget that the stories are not just told to everyone; they are told to the writer at a particular time, and then the writer prepares them for yet another audience, the reader. The stories Margay heard from Mrs. Davidson while carrying her daughter, Marin, reflect the changes in their relationship, and this is reflected in the things they discussed. If the book had been written then, instead of years earlier, it might have a slightly different emphasis. In the epilogue to the second addition, she writes about her pregnancy and daughter's birth and how that influenced the types of questions she wanted to ask Florence.

> This turning point in my own life had a considerable impact on my understanding of the life history process. In the summer of 1982, six months pregnant, I interviewed Florence regarding Haida perspectives on pregnancy. The immediacy of my own experience led me to ask numerous questions that had not occurred to me during our earlier life history interviews. As my focus turned to my young daughter in the months and years ahead, I thought often of the questions I might have asked, but had not, on Haida views of child development and child rearing. (Blackman 1992, 160)

Karen Brewster's life history of Harry Brower, *An Umialik's Life: Conversations with Harry Brower, Sr.*, illustrates the importance of the relationship between narrator and writer and the importance of the particular time in each person's life when they come together to work. Karen, a young single woman working at the Inupiat History, Language and Culture Commission in Barrow, was eager to learn Inupiaq culture. She had time after work and on weekends to spend with elders. Harry, a respected elder, whaling captain, and spokesperson on issues facing the community, had lived a full life, and now, as old age was slowing him down, he also had time. Harry realized that in Karen there was a person who cared deeply about the community and about the cultural ways and someone who wanted to learn. They became good friends, and their relationship is the basis for his sharing stories with her. Karen writes:

> In Harry, I found the instructor I had been seeking. There were other Inupiat elders who also could have provided this information, but Harry happened to be one of the first I met and was someone with whom I was immediately comfortable. I quickly became an eager student.
>
> The timing was obviously right for Harry as well. He was an older man who could no longer go out traveling and hunting like he had in his younger days. His health problems kept him close to home. He now had time to spend sitting around the house in the evening telling stories, hours which otherwise would have been spent hunting ducks, setting a fishnet, checking a trapline, cleaning fox skins, feeding a dog team, preparing whaling gear, or caring for his family. (Brewster 1998, 14–15)

Their relationship is marked not just by mutual interests but also by the unique time in their lives when they came together to work. They both had time and an interest in sharing.

The stories that Harry shared were shaped by Karen's questions, and her understanding of the public role that he played in key events on the Arctic Slope—petroleum exploration and scientific research on whale populations. The manuscript also reflects Harry's deep spiritual beliefs about the whales and his relationship with them. In sharing this information with Karen, he demonstrated trust that she would be able to present this correctly to a larger audience, that she knew both what he meant and what the audience would need to

know in order to understand. This level of trust put a big responsibility on Karen's shoulders. I think the strength of the book lies in
Karen's willingness to expose herself as part of the story and her
skills in creating context for Harry's stories so they can be retold to
a larger audience of readers unfamiliar with Eskimo life.

Krupat (1983, 262) makes the important point that life histories
are a foreign genre for Native Americans. There aren't cultural traditions of people telling the story of their lives to each other. For Native
Americans life histories are a product of oral history interviews and are
not part of their oral traditions. They are a reconstruction. For
instance, in the Moses Cruikshank book, I worked from the stories
Moses told about his life and linked stories together that followed the
connections he often made. This flows nicely, but I also employed
chapter breaks and subheadings to indicate changes and places where
there aren't links. In Waldo Bodfish's book, I worked from a list of stories about people and events that he had told about before. I asked
him to retell the stories. Then I pieced them together chronologically.

I can't imagine an evening of storytelling in which Moses or
Waldo would repeat all of the stories in the way I retold them, yet as
life histories these provide the reader with a coherent view of each
person's life and some of the themes that influenced it. Viewed this
way, life histories are constructs; albeit constructed from "life stories," they are free-flowing constructs of meaning by a teller, largely
unhindered by questions or prompting (Titon 1980) but edited,
contextualized, and organized for a reading audience by a writer.

It is the illusion of life story that we try to create in the oral biography, drawing on the freshness of the teller's voice to make it appear
that the entire construct is their meaning from page one to the end,
as if we, the readers, are seated at the teller's feet as they weave a
story with themes and subthemes that convey a deep sense of who
they are. And of course, as Chase Hensel has pointed out to me, the
writer does not want the reader to focus on the scaffolding but
instead to feel like they are listening to the narrator.

The classic oral biographies employ this technique quite effec-
tively. Consider *Sun Chief* (Talayesva 1942), *Crashing Thunder*
(Blowsnake 1983), *Mountain Wolf Woman* (Lurie 1961), or *All God's
Dangers: The Life of Nate Shaw* (Rosengarten 1974). The goal in these
works is to convey a sense of the person through the way they represented themselves to the writer. As we have seen in Karen Brewster
and Margay Blackman's work, one way to immerse the reader into

the life of the narrator is to describe the relationship between writer and narrator, thereby creating a bridge for the reader. In these cases, the narrator becomes more than a conveyor of information, and we, the reading audience, by familiarity with both the writer and narrator, are invited into the discussion. We are reminded of Ruth Behar's relationship with Sanapia and the causes they shared. In this case, the book is truly as much about Ruth as about Sanapia (Behar 1993). While the balance of voices and focus can be tricky, the goal is to get the reader to imagine what the writer is saying. So, knowing the way the writer learns and knows what the narrator says is important. It is also important to know the interests of the writer and how these influenced the narrator's choice of topics to discuss.

The two most common reasons for writing life histories are to portray the events and experiences of an extraordinary person and to emphasize a person whose life illustrates the experiences and history of others in the region. In the first case, of an individual who has brought about change, it could be a great warrior or sage—a man like Black Elk (Jackson 1990)—or it could be a person who is out of the limelight but plays a pivotal role in the community—a woman like Sadie Brower Neakok. Sadie, the subject of Margay Blackman's oral biography (1989), grew up the daughter of Charles Brower, a powerful trader in Barrow. She had a Western education but also learned the ways of her mother, an Inupiaq woman known for her generosity. As an adult, Sadie distinguished herself as a magistrate and was known for her ability to find common ground between the Western legal system and the cultural values of the Eskimo community. She is an extraordinary person.

The second common reason for an oral biography is to feature an individual whose life exemplifies the history of a region or people and the particular conditions experienced by a culture or subculture. A good example of this is Sharon Gmelch's book, *Nan, an Irish Tinker Woman*. Nan was not an extraordinary person, but her life illustrates many of the experiences of poor Irish folk who first made their living on the backroads of Ireland, doing small jobs for farmers. They were known for their tinsmithing ability and for dealing in horses. With the industrial revolution, urbanization, and mechanization, their labor was no longer needed. Their way of life had little to offer in the modern state; in fact, they became a nuisance to others. In Nan's life, we come to appreciate a person who both lived that traditional life and experienced the transition from traveling to settled life. The book portrays the difficulties she faced as she tried to adapt. As we come to know her, we come to appreciate the plight of a whole group of people.

Life histories have been used by anthropologists interested in enculturation and cultural adaptation to change. Charles Hughes's study *Eskimo Boyhood* (1974) is about the life of a young boy growing up on St. Lawrence Island in the 1930s and 1940s. Hughes' work on St. Lawrence Island was preceded by that of Dorothea and Alexander Leighton, his teachers. The Leightons were psychiatrists who developed an interest in how life histories could help them understand the mental health of their patients. We have an interesting window into their work through interviews with Dorothea. I hope someday to complete, in collaboration with Barbara Glatthorn and others, a life history of Dorothea.

The Leightons' interest in life history led them to Columbia University where Ralph Linton and Abram Kardiner were pioneering the field of culture and personality studies. The Leightons became interested in this area because of their earlier training with Adolph Meyer, a psychiatrist who used life stories as a way to treat patients suffering from mental illness. Dorothea told me a bit about Dr. Meyer:

> And then he went on to New York City where he continued working with patients, and began to build kind of a way of thinking about people with psychiatric problems. He kept on with his technique of getting people to tell him their life experience, their families, living, and whatever else they mentioned . . . I think that Dr. Meyer's point of view was undoubtedly the reason that we got the idea that we wanted to collect some life stories. (Glattham 5 n.d., 29–31)

The Leightons felt that the approach could be expanded in many different cultural settings. Their basic interest was to understand the range of life experiences and the types of experiences and practices that contributed to or detracted from mental health. This fit in quite well with the direction of the seminars that were held at Columbia. Dorothea explained it this way:

> I guess there were between ten and twenty people who met bi-weekly or monthly, I forget which, in New York City. As far as I remember, Dr. Meyer had been notified of this, and when we told him of our interest to look at unfamiliar people, he suggested that we attend . . . The topic under discussion was the relationship, if any, between culture

and personality. In other words, if you knew about culture, would you be able to predict the personality of its members" (Glatthorn n.d., 37)

Their contacts with Linton and Clyde Kluckhohn led them to the Navajo Reservation in 1940 and then to St. Lawrence Island, where they worked with Eskimo people. The Alaska work has been of particular interest because the life stories she collected and edited provide a window into life on the island during that period. We come to appreciate a variety of personalities and a range of issues and concerns that different people were dealing with at that time (Leighton and Leighton 1983).

Leighton's work and subsequent studies have demonstrated that the life history approach can give us, the students of oral narrative, a way to discern how cultural patterning influences, but doesn't determine, human thought and action. As more studies have been done, the sheer volume of information has helped broaden this appreciation. Consider, for instance, the striking differences between the life and thoughts of Crashing Thunder, whose story was told to Paul Radin (Blowsnake 1983), and the story of Mountain Wolf Woman, his sister, which was recorded by Nancy Lurie in 1958, thirty-two years after Radin's work with Crashing Thunder was first published in 1926. One of Lurie's intents was to demonstrate how different this woman's life was from her brother's (Lurie 1961).

These two life histories are further reminders that the life recalled by a teller and scripted for readers by a writer is a mere foggy glimpse of a life, a construct at best. Beyond such a collection of stories lie people who depend upon their understanding of others and their skills as storytellers to make sense and convey meaning to a broader audience. The communication takes time and a spirit of openness.

Life histories are a good way to get at basic lessons of life because the teller is asked to relate a lifetime of experiences in a relatively short amount of time and to generalize about what lessons they've learned. Attitudes are evident in the content of their comments and in how they present themselves. For instance, in the life history of Mary Peterson, a healer from Kodiak, we come to understand the pain she has experienced and the ways she has coped with hardship. Out of this story emerges a message of strength, how she learned to cope and overcome and become an example for others. Considerable credit also goes to the writer-compiler, Joanne Mulcahy, who does an exquisite job of painting the context and arranging the individual stories. For instance, the book begins with a gripping episode in which Mary is seeking shelter. Immediately the reader is immersed in her problems and has a basis from which to appreciate the evolution of her life to the present.

Sometimes the messages in a life history can be quite subtle, and we have to know the tellers well in order to understand what they really mean. In Moses' book, *The Life I've Been Living* (Cruikshank 1986), and in Howard's book, *My Own Trail* (Jackson 1998), these men use stories to convey messages about how they think people should live and the consequences when we don't follow the messages embedded in the stories. I firmly believe that Moses and Howard used the recording context to convey not only what they did but their code of life. I did not realize this at first, but as I lived with these stories and saw how the men used them in different situations, I came to this understanding. At the time, this was a startling discovery because others who had read the books weren't talking about the life histories in this way. I remind myself that stories are meant to have life, to be lived with (to borrow from Julie Cruikshank). Our understanding should grow as we apply the stories to the situations we face. Ironically, I had to analyze and label the stories to understand this; for others, maybe the stories just sink in over time and become an awareness that guides action and interpersonal dealings. Certainly people respect Moses and Howard for the way they live and what they represent. That's because they know them. But what about those people who don't know them? How well do the written stories of these man convey a sense of how to live? Perhaps this is a sober reminder that the written tradition can preserve text, but stories and lives derive their meaning from life itself, from the human struggle to determine in each new setting what is right and wrong, good and bad. Without the struggle, the wisdom in the stories and the example set by the narrators has little meaning. Life history, like other forms of oral history, can be a resource, but we must recognize connections between the stories and our lives.

The oral biography is a unique form of collaboration between teller and writer, and as we have seen in this chapter, this team works together to convey meaning in a very delicate dance. The writer seeks to preserve the voice of the teller, the teller crafts his or her meaning, and they both struggle to visualize audience members and what they need to understand what has been shared. The teller and writer perform for an unseen future audience. This performance, like the recording on the shelf, becomes frozen in time, an artifact, but hopefully it will be subject to interpretation and reinterpretation over time as the experiences of old and new readers ever create new opportunities to see the stories in a fresh light.

Harry Brower Sr. and Karen Brewster in Barrow. Harry, a respected elder with a lifetime of experiences to share, and Karen, a young woman eager to learn about Inupiaq life, formed a friendship and collaboration that was important to both of them. Photo courtesy of Karen Brewster.

part three

Issues Raised by Stories

The Whole Truth and
Nothing but the Truth

I have a poster on the outside of my office door that has a picture of Chief Peter John dressed in academic garb and next to him is a quote and a picture of a plant that is called wild potato. The quote is from Peter, speaking about the location of the University of Alaska Fairbanks.

> Troth Yeddha' is a word that comes from a long time before the whiteman came to Alaska. It means wild potato hill. Our people used to come to this hill to pick troth. They would paddle up the creek, Troth Yeddha' No', and camp by the lake, Troth Yeddha' Mene'.
>
> Troth Yeddha' was an important meeting place. The grandfathers used to talk and advise one another. When they learned this place would be used for a school, the university, they came here one last time. They decided the school would be good and would carry on a similar traditional use of the hill. The hill would continue being a place where thinking and working together happen. They placed an eagle feather on a pole. This was to let all the people know that the Dena would no longer be using the ridge for a meeting place or to pick wild potatoes. They were also giving a blessing so their grandchildren would be a part of this school. (Summary of speech given during the 1994 Rural Students Services Summit by Traditional Chief Peter John, 1997, UAF Interior-Aleutians Campus.)

This poster has prompted a great deal of discussion. One of the history professors who has studied the history of the university claims that there is nothing in the written record to substantiate that Indian elders used to meet at this spot, that they erected a pole with an eagle feather, and that they blessed the spot. He finds the poster quite distasteful because it promotes a story that the university is now touting as the truth. What we do know is that there are corroborative accounts regarding the naming of the site and the fact that people gathered here to collect the wild potatoes. So far, though, we have not been able to find in the oral or the written record mention of the elders gathering here to discuss important things or to bless the site.

I think it is important to clarify that although Peter's is the only account found so far, it might be true. Peter told this story when he was given an honorary doctorate from the university, so the site was on his mind. I personally think that the stimulation to think about the site and about education could have been the impetus for recalling what he heard and maybe saw in his lifetime. However, I also agree with the history professor that this should be qualified as Peter's story and any publicizing of it should make this qualification, at least until more information is forthcoming.

Reconstructing the Ethnographic Context

Unless we were at a performance and even sometimes when we were, we can never be sure how a person used or intended a story, but we can, when other accounts are available, compare tellings of the story by other tellers to see if there are similar themes emphasized. For instance, Howard Luke tells the story of the loon and its necklace, a popular Athabascan account, with lots of references to its telling.

Howard's account, recorded by Jan Steinbright Jackson, is about an old couple. The man is blind and the woman is stingy. She withholds food from her husband. The old man approaches a loon who offers to heal his blindness in exchange for the man's bone necklace. They agree and the loon takes the man on his back and dives under the water. After three dives the man can see perfectly well.

The old man then approaches his wife, who is drying meat. Pretending that he is still blind, he says he smells meat. When she denies this, he takes his cane and strikes her on the back with the command, "Be an ant, be an ant!" She becomes an ant (Jackson 1998, 24–25).

The anthropologist, Ingrid Johnson, recalls how her mother told this story to Catherine "Kitty" McClellan, a pioneer anthropologist who worked in the Yukon with the elder Mrs. Johnson (McClellan 1975, 170). Unfortunately, I haven't found where Kitty published the story; I only have references to it, but I do know why Ingrid retold the story. Ingrid was interviewing her mother about Kitty McClellan and their work together and was interested in the things that her mother shared with Kitty. When Ingrid talked to her mother about the interview, her mother recreated the session, including the account of the loon story (Johnson, personal communication, May 2000).

In this example, Ingrid used the story to illustrate the types of things her mother told Kitty. Howard used the story to illustrate the importance of respect. I am quite sure that Mrs. Johnson would agree with how Howard used the story, but this was probably not her intent when she told it to her daughter; her intent was to illustrate the types of things she and Kitty recorded years ago. It would be fun to know what prompted Mrs. Johnson and Kitty to record that story. The point is that in any story there is always more meaning than is explicitly expressed in the words that are spoken. We want to know why the story was told. Trouillot put the complications in this well when he said,

> If memories as individual history are constructed, even in this minimal sense, how can the past they retrieve be fixed? The storage model has no answer to that problem. Both its popular and scholarly versions assume the independent existence of a fixed past and posit memory as the retrieval of that content. But the past does not exist independently from the present. Indeed, the past is only past because there is a present, just as I can point to something *over there* only because I am *here*. (Trouillot 1995, 15)

Stories don't stand still. The loon story has also been recorded widely in Inupiaq and Inuit culture areas (Hall 1998, 245–47; Arnaktauyok 1998; Metayer 1972, 92–98; Mishler 1988, 2001).[26] We can reduce all of these versions to one theme, greediness, but this type of reduction makes us blind to how the story is used to show proper and improper relations between family members, husband and wife and, in another telling, mother and son.

Oral tradition is built on multiple tellings and cumulative processing by listeners who hear the story in different ways. It is constructed both over time and each time a story is retold. A story such as the one about the first Tanana Chiefs Conference (see chapter 6) may comprise more than what is said at any one telling. The story undoubtedly changes, but it is also true that the story told at one time may be a reference to a larger account. Unfortunately, in the case of recorded oral history, unlike storytelling, we rarely have the opportunity to ask the teller if there is more to the story; we simply have what he or she has given on tape. Unless we can consult other recordings, we are limited to the one telling. So, in the case of the Tanana Chiefs Conference, we don't know whether the recordings reflect all that the tellers wanted to convey, or whether they represent and reference a fuller account that they assume the audience at the time of the recording knew quite well.

Since most recent recordings of the Tanana Chiefs Conference story don't contradict the earlier ones, we can conclude that the outline of the story has not changed substantially. There is one notable case where Alfred Starr, a respected elder from Tanana and Nenana, provided an account that does differ in some respects from the usual interpretation. He claims the chiefs would have favored a reservation (see Schneider 1990, H5, and 1995a, 196–97). In the past, I have argued that Starr's interpretation of the chiefs' position was strongly influenced by his personal experience with reservations in the continental United States.

It is not easy to dismiss Starr's claim since his father was at the 1915 meeting, and Alfred was in an excellent position to hear about the proceedings. When I went back to the transcript of his testimony, I found an interesting clarification that I had missed before. Starr was actually claiming that the chiefs wanted a reservation *as long as* it was large enough to let them live their lifestyle, which I now interpret to mean movement from camp to camp and wide-ranging hunting areas, traplines, and fishing sites. Ownership in the sense of exclusion wasn't so much an issue as full-ranging access and some assurance that the game wouldn't be hunted out.

I'm still not sure we have resolved the question, but this new interpretation, based on the qualification of how big a reservation should be, does make Starr's testimony more consistent with the record but adds new questions about the original meeting and the transcript of the proceedings. We may never know the extent to which semantics played a part in a possible misunderstanding or how much the cultural differences in how each party conceived of land ownership and use affected the meeting and the record produced.

Then, there is the nagging question of whether Alfred Starr, in talking about the meeting years after it took place, and after his experiences outside of Alaska, was giving us his interpretation of how reservations could or might work. He was, after all, not just reporting history but interpreting it for the people present during a formal review.

In cases like this, one can argue over which accounts are true and which ones are not, but for our purposes, this can blind us to more important questions: how and why do the stories differ and in what ways can both be true?

Internal and External Tests of Validity

We start with some distinctions. David Dunaway defines the terms this way: 'Validity (how the testimony compares to other sources), reliability (whether the same question is answered the same way more than once by the source), and verifiability (whether the testimony can be authenticated)" (1991, 260).

Barbara Allen Bogart and Lynwood Montell (Allen and Mantell 1981, 71–87) remind us that there are two types of tests for validity, internal and external. We can determine the internal validity of a story by asking if the details of the story are consistent with each other, whether the story follows a logical sequence, and whether it appears that the storyteller is of sound mind. Don Ritchie (1995, 14–15, 93, 99) notes that we can further ask: Is this a firsthand or secondhand account? Are there subsequent incidents that influenced the teller's retelling? How does the storyteller explain discrepancies between his or her account and others? Quoting Arthur Schlesinger Jr., Don asks if the remarks are "plausibly supported by context or other evidence?"

External tests of a story's validity require that we compare the account with other sources. These should be found in other oral records, in the oral tradition, and in written, photographic, archaeological, and other forms of documentation. Experience and empirical tests can also confirm parts of a story. The external tests for validity are important for two reasons: to determine if the account is consistent with others and to gain cultural perspective on the story, that is, to see what elements are emphasized and perhaps find explanations of why those elements reappear.

One of the best examples of how to use external tests of validity comes from the Aleutian Islands. In 1948, William Laughlin and Gordon Marsh recorded a story of how the Aleuts had massacred Russian fur traders. They had no corroborating evidence for the story until the summer of 1970 when Laughlin discovered a mass grave. Analysis showed that the skeletal material was not Aleut. Moreover, there was cultural material in the grave that clearly linked the bodies to the Russians. This included copper boxes, coat buttons, musket balls, a finger ring, and fabric.

The final piece of evidence to emerge in this mystery was an account from 1780 that described the discovery of the massacre site by a Russian party. The remains were well enough preserved that the new party could identify their dead compatriots. The three sources—

oral tradition, archaeology, and written accounts—when taken together validate the main themes of the Aleut story (Laughlin 1980, 120–26). The pieces don't usually come together this well!

Patience and persistence are key in this work. Ernest "Tiger" Burch is one of the real masters at evaluating oral accounts and reconstructing history. The appendices to his book *The Inupiaq Eskimo Nations of Northwest Alaska* (1986) contain seven examples. In one case, he reconstructs a disaster that wiped out an entire village; in another, he determines the movement of people from one region to another. Tiger is meticulous in recording information, and like piecing together a jigsaw puzzle, he continuously works on how the evidence fits. He has done this over many years. When he discovers mistakes or when he decides the information is too incomplete to support a conclusion, as he did in some of the genealogical reconstructions for his appendices, he makes it a point to tell people about his uncertainty. We trust his judgment of the evidence not only because of how much he knows about the region, the issues, and the sources but also because he is open to correcting himself.

Sometimes, as in the following case, people interpret truth differently because they recognize different cause-and-effect relationships. Julie Cruikshank demonstrates that there are opportunities for science and oral tradition to complement each other—science providing evidence in the physical realm (empirical cause and effect) and oral tradition in the social realm of how moral relationships are believed to influence the natural world. Julie retells the story she heard from elders of how the Lowell Glacier in the Yukon advanced across the Alsek River, creating a huge lake. This backed water up to near Haines Junction. Geologists confirm that the glacier has advanced many times and built up ice, but their explanations of cause and effect differ from the Native tradition.

Kitty Smith told Julie that the glacier was called by an Athabascan shaman who had been insulted by a Tlingit visitor. The visitor mocked him by pointing out his bald head: "Ah, that old man, the top of his head is just like the place gopher plays, a bare stump." The shaman called the glacier. It created a giant lake, and when the waters rose, they burst through the glacier, scouring the land and destroying the group of Tlingit camped at the junction of the Tatshenshini and Alsek Rivers.

Julie points out that science can confirm such events and oral tradition can provide possible explanations (Cruikshank 1991, 33).

The scientific and the cultural explanations serve different ends, and each demands a different type of evaluation. If we use the same standards for both, then we lose meaning. Both agree that physical forces cause environmental change. The cultural explanation posits an ultimate cause that cannot be proved or disproved but is central to a belief system that right and wrong behavior influences the natural world. As in the loon story, the belief is that all of our world is connected and worthy of our respect. (The story of how the glacier advanced in Glacier Bay, mentioned in chapter 3, also illustrates this point.) If we were to just impose an empirical test on these stories and accept only what could be proven that way, the results would obscure the meaning and value of the stories.

In the Northern Province of South Africa, droughts are a common concern, and poor farmers depend upon sufficient rainfall each year to grow their crops and raise their cattle. In my honors history class at the University of the North, I asked students for stories about droughts in the province. I chose the subject because I knew that the farmers depended on rain and suffered a great deal because they couldn't afford irrigation systems. It seemed like a rich topic for oral history. Several of my colleagues at the library also shared stories about water. Esther Mnisi, told a story from the Northern Province, the Giyani region of South Africa. Ike Matibhe and Cecil Maqoko also contributed stories and interpretation.

Esther began her story by noting that she heard it in 1994 from a Shangaan woman. The Shangaan people at that time were experiencing a drought. The story told how the White people stole a baby snake and the mother snake retaliated by withholding water. Both White and Black farmers suffered, but the White people who owned most of the land suffered most. I asked Esther if she had heard other tellings of the story, and she said that she had; in one version from other regions of the country, it was a two headed snake that withheld the water.

Cecil told a similar story from the Western Cape, about a drought that happened in 1996. In this account, White fishermen caught the mermaid Momlambo and took it out of the water. This caused massive rain and flooding.

These two stories were followed by one told by Ike, who heard it from his father, about an event that took place in Venda. Venda is to the north of Pietersberg. There was a king who died, and his first son took over the kingship. The son "mixed the traditions" of the people with Western ways. This angered the ancestors, and they caused the stream to dry up, a drought on the land, and wars between the people. The dry streambed was strewn with stones that looked like faces. When the elders saw this they advised the king to go back to his traditions and not to follow the Western ways. The king returned to tradition, the stream was replenished, and there was peace.

This was obviously a very structured session. I asked the three people to think about drought stories, and Ike and Cecil heard Esther's story several days before our session. They had time to reflect on it before the four of us got together. Ike had even consulted his father. All of these things were part of the context, so it was quite natural that the storytellers built on each other's themes. I encouraged this by the way I asked questions, fishing for each person to analyze what had been said and share their observations. I think the dialogue was quite instructive because it gave a forum for determining common themes.

All three of my colleagues agreed that stories are a way to talk about conflicts between cultures. In each case, an apparently old belief is used to explain a modern predicament, and the Whites are in each case blamed for both the modern predicament and for disturbing a traditional order. For instance, in Esther's account the Whites who stole the snake baby cause the drought. Juxtaposed with this is another story of Whites taking the good land and imposing the policies of apartheid. The two stories come together when the teller concludes that the snake caused the drought and that those who had the largest and wealthiest farms (the Whites) suffered most. In the story by Cecil, the mermaid controlled the water, and when she was taken by Whites, she caused floods. Thus, the Whites are responsible for the flooding. In Ike's story, the ancestors register their disagreement with the young king who has taken up Western ways, which are believed to be bad for them. They withhold water and bring on wars. Once the king returns to tradition, gives up White ways, and performs the appropriate ceremonies, the ancestors are satisfied, the water comes back to the river, and there is peace. In each of these cases, water is a barometer of the people's health and well-being, and the disasters are expressed in terms of White people's wrong actions or bad influence.

In the class, I was told two other snake stories, both from Venda and both involving the taking of the baby snake by White people for use in a zoo or snake park. In these stories, the mother or parent snake is purported to be in search or pursuit of the baby and causes thunderstorms that destroy the roofs of houses. The storms are so strong that they even destroy government buildings.

For several weeks, I tried to relate these stories to the ones my colleagues had provided. I kept stumbling on the fact that in the first version the snake withheld rain, and in the stories from Venda she causes wind and thunderstorms, usually associated with rain. Do people believe that the snake can do both?

What if, instead of trying to reconcile differences, we ask about the similarities between these stories? All of the stories express a belief that an individual's improper actions can cause the snake or mermaid to perpetrate major environmental catastrophes. In each story, White people are blamed for disrupting the natural order, and there are ramifications that affect everyone. Thus, in all cases, the stories provide a somewhat indirect way to talk about Black South Africans' anger with the actions of White South Africans.

How Do We Know When We've Got It Right?

My evaluation of these stories depends upon (1) a recognition of traditional ways that people explain what causes disasters, (2) an understanding of the particular disasters discussed, and (3) a recognition of how people use stories to explain the impact of White people in South Africa. Key questions for us to ask include the following: What is the role of thunderstorms, droughts, and floods in other stories? Are they consistently moral barometers of right and wrong action? How do these stories compare with others in terms of the use of traditional beliefs to explain the impact of Whites on the lives of Black South Africans? Do the snake and mermaid appear in other stories and function in similar ways?

Such questions are fundamental to the historical record, which is incomplete without noting people's experiences and their perceptions of cause and effect. Although I am not very far along in answering these questions, the discussions with Esther, Cecil, and Ike certainly helped. I have found two written references to the role of snakes and rain in Venda society, but since one of the accounts (Miller 1979, 139) is of a popular nature and seems to be derived from an earlier, more scholarly work (Stayt 1968, 309–10), I probably have only one outside source or external form of evaluation. Stayt claims that the Venda people (BaVenda) believe that not treating the python properly during certain times of the year can cause a drought. He does not mention White people mistreating or taking the snake.

Some might argue that there should also be an empirical test of validity—that we should ask if the event described can be proven to have actually occurred. An empirical test is one that relies on evidence that lends itself to evaluation through the senses: sight, touch, taste, and smell. As we noted earlier with the glacier stories, knowledge for most people is not confined to what they know through their senses. Knowledge also consists of beliefs and values, which, though we may all agree they are worth knowing, don't lend themselves to an empirical test. There may also be disagreement by listeners about different parts of a story; some might argue for an empirical test and others claim that is inappropriate. If part of the story fails the empirical test, what about the rest of the account?

The classic Western example is the age-old arguments over interpretation of the Holy Bible. Some claim it is literally true, others that it is not, and still others claim that asking such a question diverts the listener/reader's attention away from the real meaning of biblical stories. The South African drought and flood stories, like similar Western biblical accounts, don't lend themselves very well to an empirical test. In fact, subjecting the stories to empirical confirmation could divert attention away from the reasons why people tell the stories. We can, of course, get confirmation from other sources about when and where floods and droughts occurred, but our first and most important job is to seek cultural understanding and a determination of whether an account is consistent with other oral sources.

We can't always achieve agreement on cultural understanding. The international community is still debating about what happened on Egypt Flight 900, the Boeing 767 aircraft that mysteriously went down after leaving from Kennedy International Airport in New York. When the American press came out with the report of findings that indicated an act of suicide was performed by the relief pilot, some Egyptian experts said that the prayer recorded on the voice recorder just before the crash would not have been made by an Egyptian contemplating suicide; instead it would be said when there is a crisis (*Fairbanks Daily News-Miner*, November 18, 1999, A1, A7). In this case, lots of other evidence pointed to suicide, but we are still left wondering, particularly given this cultural evidence, about what the prayer meant.

Here, Western technology and emphasis on empirical tests (decoding the flight recorder and examining the wreckage) comes face to face with a cultural explanation that does not lend itself to such a test (interpretation of how a prayer is used, even if it isn't definitive). We have the aeronautical engineer's explanation of what happened in the plane and a cultural explanation clarifying under what circumstances the prayer might have been invoked.

We hate it when we can't resolve such questions, when we have to live with not knowing. The best we can say is that certain parts of the story can appropriately be subjected to empirical tests, while for other parts it may be more important to remain open to new clues that impart meaning. This is a bit like Peter John's story about the site of the university. Some parts of the story have corroborating evidence, while other parts do not. In all cases, we must be clear about what can be proven, what exists in the realm of belief, and what must be open to continued questioning and speculation.

Issues of Representation

Chapter 9 was about getting the story right: about truth, validity, and accurate cultural interpretation. This chapter extends that discussion, because getting it right also means making sure that the way the story is retold and represented to new audiences remains true to the original intent of its telling. There is a very thin line between leaving room for new interpretation and new ways of retelling on the one hand and, on the other hand, taking a story so far from its initial or native context that the meaning the original teller and primary audience intended is lost or its portrayal in a new setting embarrasses or exposes them in an uncomfortable way.

Henry Glassie, in his classic book *Passing the Time in Ballymenone*, reminds us that making sense of what is shared in a story is a complex dance between audience, teller, and tradition. The teller bears a big responsibility not only to speak what he or she knows but also to say it with sincerity. "He must act responsibly toward himself, for if he is uncommitted to performance, if he speaks, as they say 'from the teeth out,' he stops his talent from unifying him with his tradition, himself, and those around him. Disengaged, his act is inauthentic, unethical, less than art" (1982, 145).

The musical *Jesus Christ Superstar* is an example from popular culture that illustrates how the vulnerability of stories to reinterpretation can be read in two ways. Some would argue that its interpretation and portrayal of Jesus Christ's life distort the biblical story and that its modern theater and screen renderings of scripture are so removed from the original narrative that they are both offensive and wrong. Others would argue just the opposite, that the new telling and way of telling are refreshing and relevant, a good way to keep the essence of an old story alive in our modern lives.

In chapter 5, I emphasized that oral history doesn't stand alone; it must be couched in cultural understanding, the checks and balances and subtle corrections that the people who determine the course of an oral tradition provide. They determine the appropriate range of correct interpretation, and they are the ones who will proclaim, "He's speaking through his teeth" if a telling does not get it right. Of course such judgment calls change as the group changes and as the story is applied to new situations. That's what creates both tension and opportunity.

Renato Rosaldo warns us, "Plundering other people's narratives by sifting them into degrees of facticity—time, probable, possible, false—risks misunderstanding their meanings. This simply goes back to the point that what people say is inseparable from how they say it. Another maxim: in order to grasp the message one has to work through the medium, rather than somehow skirting around or leaping directly behind it" (Rosaldo 1980, 92).

The first challenge of oral history is to determine what was meant at the time of the telling and how the storyteller used the story to create meaning. Only then can we get the story right in the retelling. At the very least, getting it right means understanding the original intent and context of telling, providing an accurate rendering in the retelling, and putting forth an honest effort to determine how a new setting and portrayal can continue to convey meaning, while staying aware of how it might be perceived by the original teller and his or her community. That's the business of the oral historian.

Creative writers, including play and screen writers, and those who work in other forms of artistic expression may take a story and recraft it to convey their message. There is nothing wrong with this; in fact it is one way new stories enter our consciousness and how old stories take on new meaning. But it is important to differentiate those efforts from the work of the oral historian who, in the interest of accuracy and sensitivity to the tellers and their communities, must create bridges between tellings and explain variations.

An oral history record is created for the future, for both people who know and those who do not know the narrator. Future audiences will benefit from as much background information as we can provide. An oral history tape or transcript is a verbatim rendering of one performance that happened to be recorded on tape or paper. It is a snapshot that may have been preserved without caption, citation, or reference (Nelson 1983b). If it is going to speak to the future it needs background and explanation.

Getting the Whole Story

In a library science class at the University of the North, Amos Makhubele, the student who told the story about the Little Big Man (see chapter 4), volunteered a narrative his grandfather had told him. The story was about how, years ago, the family was forced to leave the Pretoria area and settle where there was poorer soil. The grandfather explained that they were forced to move because of development in Pretoria. As Amos was telling the story, I kept thinking about policies of the government and wondering whether this wasn't really a story about apartheid. Amos never mentioned the word, but when he finished, I asked him.

Amos said that, for him, it was indeed a story about apartheid, but for his grandfather, who did not understand the government's policies, it was about the move to a less productive place to make a living. The grandfather used the story to tell about the family's difficult move, but the grandson, after my prompting, agreed that he sees the story as not only about the move itself but also about the government's treatment of Blacks. It is hard to judge how much my questioning influenced Amos or how his grandfather might have told the story differently to others, but the important thing now is to know the grandfather's and grandson's understandings, to be aware of my question, and to recognize how Amos uses the story and represents its meaning to later audiences.

Getting the story right means getting the whole story, and that now includes the essential parts of the dialogue between Amos and me. To ignore my input in the narrative is to cut out the role of clarification and further elaboration so common in dialogue (Tedlock 1979). Context statements are one way we can provide a fuller record.

Context Statements

Context statements provide background on a particular interview or storytelling session. Why was the person chosen? Why were the questions asked? How were they asked? How did the teller shape the interview or recording opportunity? What is the relationship between interviewer and narrator, audience and teller? Of course, a context statement just refers to one specific interview. Each new interview needs its own statement.

One of our earlier jukebox projects featured folks who lived on the Yukon River between Circle and Eagle, in an area designated the Yukon-Charley Rivers National Preserve. We wanted to interview Albert Carroll because he was a riverboat captain and ran a barge service. We thought he would give listeners a picture of life on the river. The interview proved to be important for many reasons, but of particular interest were his descriptions of barging freight. He is one of the few remaining people who can talk about a small-time freighting operation, the stops on the river, and the types of goods they carried. We didn't expect it, but one of the things that Albert mentioned was the amount of fuel they had to haul to the gold mining operation at Woodchopper and how his operation was influenced by ups and downs in the mining industry (H91-22-59, Oral History Collection, Elmer Rasmuson Library).

We chose Albert because of his knowledge of piloting, but we were pleasantly surprised to get additional information about other businesses on the river. In our context statement, we noted our original interest and the understanding that he was able to provide. The context statement indicates what we hoped for: background on his family, piloting, and trapping. Unfortunately, we neglected to mention his perspectives on business along the river and the importance of Woodchopper to his barge operation. It is a necessary addition because it points to a key feature of the interview and a new (at least for us) account of river business. This is the original context statement, with what I consider the necessary additional information in italics.

Albert Carroll was interviewed by Dan O'Neill and William Schneider at the house of Owen Stockbridge in Central, Alaska. Owen traps with Albert and has also worked on the river barges with him. Albert and Owen were taking a break from woodcutting. Owen is present during the interview and comments when Albert asks him about dates. Owen also shared some pictures from the trapping camp he and Albert use in the Johnson Gorge area of the Kandik River.

Albert speaks about his experience piloting boats on the Yukon River and its tributaries and about trapping. He speaks from the perspective of a lifelong user of the area. As a child, he accompanied his parents on their trips up the Yukon River from Fort Yukon and up the Kandik River, portaging with them over to the Black River.

Albert's father, James, was a White trapper and, later, a storeowner in Fort Yukon. He is author of the book, *First Ten Years in*

Alaska. Albert's mother, Fanny, was an Athabascan from the Fort Yukon-Porcupine River area.

Albert provides an interesting perspective on the Woodchopper mining operation and how their fuel needs influenced his barge business.

The added information alerts the listener to another reason, beyond the obvious ones, why the interview is important and how it contributes to the overall collection of recordings on the Yukon-Charley area.

Context statements should also reflect the interviewer's interviewing style and position relative to the interview. This gives future listeners a way to evaluate how the interviewer influences the course of the interview. Again as part of the Yukon-Charley interviews, my colleague Dan O'Neill and I recorded some administrators who were in positions of power at the time the preserve was established. In our context statements, we noted that I worked for the National Park Service during this period, knew many of the people well, and was involved in formulation of policy. Dan, on the other hand, had no connection with the Park Service and, while less personally informed, was a more objective interviewer and had a more thorough knowledge of some of the written sources. We did many of the interviews together, and the sessions reflect our different backgrounds and our different ways of seeking information—I asked open-ended questions whereas his were more directed and, some would say, confrontational. He is fond of what he calls the "impertinent question."[27] In some interviews, our strategy included a "good guy" open-ended questioner and a "tough guy" interrogator. At one point, after an exasperating interview, Dan decided life was too short to take that much heat, so we decided to let me take the lead with the hard questions. He recalls: "I still couldn't hold myself back . . . If Bill wasn't asking the tough one, I still felt I had to pipe up and throw it in there" (H91-22-60, side 2, Oral History Collection, Elmer Rasmuson Library). This quote is from an interview with both of us about the interviews. It gives you a sense for our different styles. In retrospect, I think we could have done a better job explaining our differences to future listeners in each context statement.

Context statements should also reflect how the interviewee, or teller, used the interview or recording session to convey what is important to them. Sometimes this will be obvious enough to the listener, sometimes not. At the Communities of Memory storytelling session in Kotzebue, Alaska, an old man born in 1903, Levi Mills, took the opportunity to tell how he worked as a heavy equipment operator during World War II and built airfields. At one point, he told about his assignment to a base out in the Aleutians, where he learned that he was working on a strip for an important plane. He now believes that he might have helped build a strip that was used by an airplane carrying one of the atomic bombs dropped on Japan. As the audience listened to his story, it was clear that he was struggling with his involvement in those events, wanting to have done the right thing for his country but also questioning the impact of the bombing. He concluded by saying, "My intentions were fulfilled, thank God! That's my story" and then broke down in tears. Immediately, there was a generous outpouring of support by the audience and reassurance that he truly had helped his country and had saved lives (Communities of Memory, Kotzebue, March 1, 1996).

It was quite an experience to hear this old man's story and to hear the audience try to assure him that he had not acted wrong, that he had done the right thing. He used the recording opportunity to express his personal turmoil, to show how a distant war affected him, and to review how he has lived with his small, but to him, significant role. (The base may never have been used by aircraft carrying atomic warheads.) The impact of his story was increased by his old age, how long he had lived with his ambivalence, and the show of support from the audience. He was not the only one who told about the pain and guilt that soldiers carry. This was the session where Vietnam veterans recounted their experiences and how hard it was to return home to loved ones who did not know or understand what they had gone through during the war (see chapter 3).

While there is some discussion of this man's story in my evaluation of the session (1996), there is no official context statement. A context statement would describe how the old man used the opportunity to express his concern, the impact of his account on the audience and its response, and how it fit with other stories that were told. Such information would help future generations more fully understand his story.

Representing the Recording in Culturally Appropriate Ways

We don't have to rely just on text. The context of an interview can also be preserved with photographs, maps, and music. If future listeners also have these images and sounds before them, they should be able to visualize and identify with the story better, much as the listener-recorder did at the time it was told.

This was dramatically illustrated to me in my work with Moses Cruikshank. We were choosing illustrations for his book and needed a sketch of a pack dog (1986, 69). The artist's rendering had the pack too low on the dog's back. Moses said this would not be comfortable for the dog, and it would not be able to work well. We had to find an old-fashioned dog pack, get it on a dog, and take a picture. Then we took the picture to the artist to redo the sketch. The accuracy of the drawing was particularly important because Moses had described in his story how the pack should fit. I was particularly concerned because of my earlier work with his father-in-law, Turak Newman. Turak didn't like some of the sketches in his book because he felt they weren't accurate (Schneider 1987, 36–37).

Many of our recordings are now loaded onto computer hard drives and CDs. There are about four hundred hours now available in electronic format. The computer technology lets us present visuals and music with text and spoken narrative. This is a very important capability because it enhances the listener-viewer's visualization of the story. For instance, to illustrate an interview with Millie Gray from Bettles, Alaska (part of the Gates of the Arctic Jukebox), we copied some of her photographs and included them in a computer file linked to her recording (H93-15-46, Oral History Collection, Elmer Rasmuson Library). The pictures of her father and mother, of the boats her father used for freighting, and of making barges add a visual dimension to her story about life on the Koyukuk River.

In a jukebox program from Southeast Alaska, we used a series of photos made by a long- time Japanese resident of Yakutat, Fhoki "Shoki" Kayamori (Kayamori–Yakutat Collection, Juneau, Alaska State Library). The images are described by two women, and their descriptions are windows into cannery operations, special events in town, and Tlingit ceremonies in the pre-WWII era. They create connections to the experiences of the older people who are featured in the oral history recordings.

Maps can also be used as reference by listeners to a speaker's story. In a project at Katmai National Park, we interviewed two women talking about a lake where they grew up. Their recounting of events around the lake became part of a jukebox project in which we keyed their descriptions to numbers on a map. When you click on a number, you can hear them tell about the place.

These photos illustrating Millie Gray's interview show her father's boat building operation. Photos courtesy of Millie Gray.

A young Elaine Abraham in the home of Japanese
photographer Fhoki Kayamori. Photo 55-611, courtesy of the Alaska State Library Historical Collections.

During the Yukon-Charley project mentioned earlier, we took photographs of signs made at the time the National Park Service began studying the area. The signs expressed the community's resistance to federal management. They were described by Jean Boone, but to actually see and read them gives viewers a stronger sense of the past and how the community responded. Seeing these old pictures makes the strong feelings many people had and still have about the actions taken by the government all the more real to the listener.

One of the most recent attempts to build context was initiated by Jarrod Decker of our Oral History Office at the University of Alaska Fairbanks. In a project based on interviews from Tatitlek, a small community in Prince William Sound, quite near to where the *Exxon Valdez* hit Bligh Reef, he decided to use cultural symbols (logos, a hunting hat, sea otter carvings, seal gut bags, and bidarkas) as background for individual pages of the jukebox program. Other staff members now use this approach routinely to convey cultural context—for instance, a historical couch-fabric pattern as a background screen to the Russian bishop's house in Sitka, a devil's club backdrop to convey medicinal plant content in an interview with a woman in Nanwalek, and a kayak backdrop for an interview with a man who describes seal hunting.

In each of these cases, the visuals support the oral narrative and reinforce the settings where the story is told and where the events described took place. The computer allows us to do these things, but it also raises ethical issues about how we represent people and the level of public exposure they are willing to accept. In each case, the addition of elements presupposes that the person interviewed and their community agree to have their information made public in these ways and that the overall message that we convey is accurate for multiple audiences of listeners and viewers.

The computer is wonderful because it allows us to add photos, maps, sound, and moving images, but with the new opportunities comes the responsibility to ensure that the representation is culturally appropriate. In Southeast Alaska, Ken Austin developed a program based on recordings from our oral history collection. For his opening screen, he chose two clan songs to introduce the program and to pay recognition to the participants. His choice of songs and the balance of different clan interests made the program inviting and immediately recognizable to Southeast Alaska Natives, but it also demanded that Ken be very sure that the choices and way people were pictured was culturally appropriate.

Since Ken's project was both for Tlingit people and for the general public, he had to provide enough background information for non-Native viewers and listeners to visualize what he was presenting and why. Visualization, the ability to relate what we hear and see to our personal experience, is key to understanding what the teller means. In cross-cultural contexts, this is particularly hard because communication is based on common experience. In essence, the supporting material that Ken and others provide on their projects creates common ground so that the recordings can be understood and appreciated by multiple audiences.

Getting the story right then is not just a matter of how we understand what was said. It is also a matter of how we communicate the story to multiple new audiences. While it is clear that photos, maps, and music can give future listeners multiple ways to relate to the story, the representations must be sensitive to cultural concerns. It is also important to remind ourselves that for all of our efforts, this is not the original telling. It is our representation of the telling.

Getting it right, then, goes beyond the details of the story, the words, to a concern with how the story is communicated to others and used to convey meaning. This means keeping the needs of particular audiences in mind. In oral history, where the teller is not present at the retelling, there should be enough supporting material to be sure the listeners or viewers can visualize the story in their minds.

Intellectual Property Rights and the Public Unfinished Business

A few years ago, I was approached by one of my Yup'ik colleagues who had just attended a writer's workshop for people who wanted to write children's books. She was upset because the participants talked about what a rich resource Native stories were for writers. She was offended because, in her region, stories are not individually owned; they are commonly known and shared, and it is offensive for someone to claim authorship. Her question to me was "Bill, what about the tapes in the library. Are they available for anyone to use? Could writers come and take these stories and claim authorship?"

The quick answer is yes. In our oral history program, if there is a release form signed by the teller, it makes the recording available to the public. The more complicated response is that the management of the tape is subject to the conditions outlined on the release form, which could include stipulations on how the recording is used, but for the recording to be in a public archive, it must be accessible to anyone. There can't be any form of censorship based on the user's background.[28] Most of the release forms for our oral history collection do not have restrictions, and the donor relinquishes to the university all rights to the recording. We make them freely available to researchers. From the standpoint of the archive, this is the easiest way to administer the collection; we avoid the possibility of lawsuit, and when someone uses the recording in a culturally insensitive way, we are legally not responsible. But where does our ethical responsibility end? How far should or can we go toward influencing how the recording is used? Who determines who owns cultural knowledge and what should be public? What role should individuals and cultural groups play in management of public collections? The following discussion begins with the Western legal basis for release agreements and copyright, and I then describe how we are trying to shape that legal tradition to meet the concerns of a cross-cultural audience.

The Release Form

The main purpose of the release form is to express in writing the agreement reached between the narrator, the interviewer, and the archive. The form gives the archive rights to make the recording available and defines the conditions for doing so. In order to make the recording public, the archive needs to control the item's copyright or have an agreement of some sort that stipulates permission to let people have access to it. Without one of these, the archives has no authority to manage the recording.

Since the interview is the product of both the interviewee and the interviewer, both parties have rights that need to be considered. Unfortunately, many release forms only have a signature line for the interviewee. The form should include signature lines for the interviewee, interviewer, and a representative of the institution that agrees to hold and manage the recording.

The release form for the University of the North Oral History Program in South Africa includes signature lines for the narrator (interviewee), the interviewer, and a representative of the university library. This form is produced in triplicate so that all parties have a copy for their files. Recently we revised our release form at the Rasmuson Library (appendix A). It tries to anticipate future forms of electronic access. An explanation sheet describing conditions and policy was developed by Robyn Russell as an aid to interviewees and interviewers (appendix B).

The release form should have space provided to specify special conditions. A common restriction is to seal the interview from access for a period of time. I recommend that this period be of minimal length, with an option to reseal if the parties feel it is necessary. Sometimes, interviews are restricted from use in media productions. Some people do not want the recording quoted directly or have objections to it being reproduced in its entirety (such as the above example of Yup'ik stories used as sources for children's books). In such cases, the contributor's wishes can be accommodated by informing users and, further, by asking them to sign statements agreeing to the conditions. These statements should be kept on file with the release forms in the archive. The archive normally cannot enforce the restriction, but it can inform users and maintain a record that they have been informed. I can't recall any collections where we have been asked to go as far as obtaining such statements from users.

In most cases, donors are satisfied that we just inform people that uses such as extraction of entire text, media broadcast, and electronic access are not permitted. These restrictions are usually the extent of donors' concerns. Certain types of restrictions should be avoided in a public archive. For example, the interviewee or interviewer should not be given the right to approve or deny access and use by particular groups or individuals.

The question of slander also has implications for archives in the United States. If a recording has information that is damaging to the character of another and the information is not substantiated, then the interviewee, interviewer, and the archive can all be held accountable (Ritchie 1995, 154; Neuenschwander 1993, 10–16). This is a strange ruling, but it means that the archive must assume responsibility to ensure that recordings in its collection are free of slander.

Given past experience, I caution against accepting donations of large collections that come without release forms. It is always hard to secure such forms after the fact; donors can help with contacts, but one should avoid putting donors in the position of negotiating a release form for the archive. For donated collections, the best situation is to have the researcher, interviewer, and/or donor work with the oral history staff before interviewing begins, so they know what the archives can and can't do in the way of restrictions. That way they can explain the conditions to the people they interview at the time they make the recording. I have argued that archives should avoid being storage closets and should only acquire materials that can be processed in a timely manner. Needless to say we have collections that have never been processed. Despite heroic staff efforts, many of these remain hopelessly lost in the administrative backlog, almost always because there are no release forms.

On the one hand, the archive is asked to be sensitive to local interests about how a recording should be managed and to know the interviewee's and interviewer's original intent and sentiment in creating a public record. I must continually remind myself that stories, even stories on tape, are not resources to be mined for information. They are each the result of a purposeful sharing with another person at a particular time. On the other hand, as a public office, the archive must secure its legal position so that it has rights to make recordings available to all future users and can ensure that the archive is not held liable in cases where a user abuses access to a recording by doing such things as misquoting, misinterpreting what was said, or presenting it in a media production despite restrictions. So, more and more, archivists must develop continuing relationships with donors and tailor management of archives to accommodate cultural concerns. At the same time, we find it necessary to be as clear as possible about what a public facility can and can't do.

In what for me was a disappointing development, we recently gave up a large and important collection. The collection is the life's work of a prominent and important researcher. The issue revolved around release forms. She wanted us to hold and care for the collection until the elders' council from the region could decide which of the recordings to make public. Some of the recordings were over ten years old, and she wanted us to copy them as a way to ensure adequate preservation. Neither of these requests are unreasonable, but as a program, my staff and I decided not to invest the time and resources on a collection that we might in the end not get rights to make publicly available.

This was unfortunate because I believe that, particularly in cross-cultural settings, public institutions are going to be asked more and more to provide safe storage for collections and to counsel groups on the pros and cons of putting their recordings into the public record. It would be a lot easier if we had dedicated resources (space and staff time) for this new direction, but we don't. So the decisions are much harder and involve giving up other things, such as the processing of existing collections for which release forms are on hand or can be easily acquired. We're not ready to do that.

During the mid-1980s, at a time of severe budget cuts in the state of Alaska, our archives acquired some collections that had letters of transmittal but did not have specific releases for each recording. This proved particularly troublesome in the case of material from the NANA Native Corporation, in Northwest Alaska. The elders in the NANA Region claimed that some of the recordings belonged to them and that they had just loaned them to the agency that then donated them to us. In the end, we had to relinquish these recordings back to the NANA people, and the whole issue created an erosion of trust. They were angry we had their recordings and felt we were slow to recognize and return them. In this case, it was an honest mistake on our part, but it points to the problems that occur when there isn't a close working relationship between the interest groups.

In another case, we hold copies of a very large collection of recordings that were made at the time of the Native land claims (mid

1970s on into the 1980s), recordings with elders who described historic sites in their home regions. These recordings were made by representatives of two federal agencies. From a legal standpoint it could be argued that the recordings, by virtue of federal money, are part of the public record subject to the Freedom of Information Act. On the other hand, the recordings were made for a specific purpose— Native corporation selection of historic and cemetery sites. It was not clear to interviewees in the early years of this project that their tapes would someday be in an archive and publicly available. That wasn't even part of the thinking of the interviewers. Technically, the federal government paid for and owns the recordings, and thus legally controls the information on the tapes. But we still need to consider the narrators, and without statements from them or their next of kin, it is hard to know how they want recordings of their words managed.

This situation is complicated by several facts: Many of the people interviewed are no longer living, so who should decide for them how their recordings are to be managed? The villages and the regions also have interests in the management of the recordings since the information is about land that is important to them. The elders weren't just speaking about their experiences. In some cases, the conditions under which the recordings were made are unclear, and there is room for misinterpretation of information. One has to imagine how disorienting it was for elders flown by helicopter to historic sites. In some cases, the interviewers were inexperienced, and interviews conducted through translators created another level of possible confusion. Language differences lead to some confused and misleading information on the recordings (Drozda 1995).

This project can teach us a great deal about what should have been done differently, and since I was part of the research effort in the early years when the problems started, I can see how shortsighted and ignorant we were about the record we were gathering. Fortunately, this collection has support from the Bureau of Indian Affairs, and there are researchers working with it to determine as much as possible about the recordings and to work with Native organizations on how the collection should be managed.

These examples point out that recordings in an archive are subject to the concerns of at least five different interest groups: the interviewee, the interviewer, the community, the archive that manages the collection, and future users. The collections curator sits in the middle. This is a challenge. It's hard to create a five-way win-win agreement.

Interests of the Cultural Group

To understand the interests of a group of people in a recording, we have to determine who is part of the group (clan, other members of the extended family, the community), and then we have to look at the meaning of the recording. I think it is fair to say that the most important thing with cross-cultural oral history collections is to ensure that there is enough information provided so future users can understand what the narrators meant, in terms of both content and intended use. Without such understanding, the recordings may be used incorrectly or in a way that is embarrassing or insulting. Some information is private. For instance, in South Africa, the knowledge shared with initiates in circumcision schools is not to be made public and does not belong in a public archive.

In Southeast Alaska, we recently had a case where an elder told about clan origin stories. Even though it seemed to me he was just providing the outlines of the stories, the clan leaders felt this was inappropriate because the clan determines who can tell the story. They said he only had the rights to tell his own clan's stories. Even with his own clan's stories, there was a question about our rights to reproduce the stories in a jukebox program for others to hear. We returned the recording to the narrator and conducted another interview with him that did not touch on clan history.

Then there are issues that should be public but only with great care in how they are retold. Consider, for instance, the production by South African Broadcasting on the death and mutilation of Chief Makgoba (*African Mysteries: The Head of Makgoba*). Chief Makgoba refused to submit to the Boer government, so they hired Swazi tribesmen to hunt him down and kill him. To prove that they had done the job, the hunters cut off his head and delivered it to the Boers. This is a complicated story that is still unfolding. The portrayal of the story by the South African Broadcasting Company made a joke of the beheading. They didn't realize it, but they made a serious mistake. The filmmakers had access to Professor Louis Changuion and his research that depicts the sensitivity of the issue, but in the act of filming they created a record that portrayed the event in an insensitive, cavalier way. Africans worship ancestors and believe they influence the lives of the living. To treat any death and burial lightly is to invoke the anger of the ancestors. This story of Makgoba should never have been reported in such a lighthearted way.[29]

Types of Community Control

In recent years there has been growing interest in finding ways to involve communities in managing collections. Two examples come to mind. Several years ago, I met with the Denakkanaaga elders. Denakkanaaga is an organization of Interior Alaska Athabascan elders. At that meeting one of the members requested that the archive at the University of Alaska Fairbanks find a way to get recordings from his home village, Minto, back to the community.

Fortunately, we got support for what became known as the Minto Documentary Project, and it produced a wealth of information about photos, tapes, films, and other primary sources relating to the community. One copy of the inventory was deposited in Minto, and one copy remains at the Oral History Office. As part of this work, we were able to copy all of the oral recordings about Minto from our collection and give the copies of tapes and the inventories of other primary sources back to the community.

Despite the immediate value of returning these materials, there are nagging problems. For instance, we gave recordings to the community that don't have release forms. In time, we may find that individuals don't want to sign a release, that they don't want us to have the recordings, and further, that they don't even want the community to have them. Nevertheless, we decided to make copies of the entire collection (those with and those without release agreements) and to give all of the copies to the community. On those recordings for which we don't have releases, we placed a label to signal that conditions for using the recording are not settled. This approach gives the community control of the copies. The originals remain in the archive and are available to the public according to each release agreement. If a tape without an agreement is requested, we do not provide it to the patron until we secure a release from the narrator or, in case of death, a close member of the family. At the university, the release form sets our use policy. In the community, we don't know if anyone will secure a release form before using a recording that does not have one. The label is a stop sign, but there is no curator controlling access. Obviously, this is not a perfect solution since it depends on the community working with individuals or their families to get releases when certain tapes are requested, and there is no mechanism to coordinate with our office on new releases. So, recordings without agreements remain in limbo.

The second example comes from a panel discussion of archivists and First Nations' people in Whitehorse, Yukon Territory, Canada, at a joint conference of the Association of Canadian Archivists and the Ruperts Land Colloquium (June 1, 1996). The session was titled "Words are Not Enough" and was a panel discussion on archival programs and community-based research and heritage preservation in the North. The topic was management of collections of recordings of Native, or First Nations, people. One of the archivists on the panel described how they house a collection of recordings from the Inuvialuit people. He went on to describe how before anyone could use the collection, the research project had to be approved by a council of Inuvialuit. I was shocked by this policy, and I tried to get clarification. The Inuvialuit panel member related that the policy developed because the Inuvialuit felt that their material had been taken away for years and that it was time to regain control of collections.

I shared this story with a group of Native colleagues in Alaska and was surprised again to hear that they were supportive of that archive's policy of Inuvialuit review and that they did not see the issue of censorship as an overriding consideration. This is a small sample size but it does indicate the frustration Native people feel for the way their histories have been collected, the way they are currently managed, and the way they are used by researchers. To some people, these issues seem to be more serious than the danger of censorship and the long-term impact on freedom of information and inquiry. I am sympathetic with their concerns about how the information has been used and represented in the past, but I am not in agreement with public archives holding collections that certain individuals may be restricted from using. For instance, if a researcher has a reputation for portraying a group of people in an unfavorable light, the group might want to restrict his or her access. This would set a serious, negative precedent that could affect scholarship and, in the long run, the community's understanding of its history.

Fortunately, there is room for a distinction between access and interpretation on the one hand and issues of how the information is represented in publications and the media on the other. If the issue is the format for reporting rather then the content, then this could be stipulated in a release form without censoring the researcher's access. As described earlier, the form can specify that the material is not to be reproduced directly in film or radio. The release could set up conditions for quotation, limiting the length or even stipulating that direct quotes are not to appear. It can even stipulate that the interviewee's name not appear. Of course, an archive can only inform users of the restrictions; it can't police them.

Jim Magdanz has put into practice a different approach. He designed a release form to be used in a research project with people on the Kobuk River. The form and explanation sheet explores possible ways the recording could be used and gives the interviewee the chance to choose options. One option invites the narrator to retain and register copyright for the recording in his or her own name. Jim explains that a narrator's copyright can work like that in any publication; it can allow free access with provisions for fair use in quotes and references.

This approach might work for public collections, if there are legal guarantees that the archive can continue to hold recordings and make them available to the public without liability. Since the recording is the product of interviewee and interviewer and hence both initially own it, unless it was completed as work for hire, it might be best if they jointly registered and held copyright. A big question is whether release agreements would still be sufficient to allow archives to hold and make recordings available to the public or whether a transfer of copyright is the only way to guarantee the archive can legally make decisions about the recording and avoid being blamed for someone misusing the recording. Without copyright, the archive could be put in a position where they had to give the recordings back to the narrator or their designate. If narrators and interviewers decide they want to end the agreement, then the tapes would have to be de-accessioned. When a collection is de-accessioned, it represents a loss in time and money spent for processing. It also means that the catalog of holdings, a document shared universally, must be changed to reflect the transfer of holdings.

Many of these issues can be solved if we spend more time with interviewees before the tape recorder is turned on to explore potential future uses and describe what the archive can reasonably provide in the way of restrictions. But the process doesn't end when the interviewer leaves with a signed release form in hand. The issues must be continually discussed and reevaluated, and curators of collections must be open to new ways to accommodate concerns. This rightfully must remain an open and unfinished chapter.

Complications of the Electronic Age

The impersonal technological invention, the computer, has forced us to examine the most personal ways people share stories and to see new ways to preserve the context of that sharing with photos, maps, text, and video. This was in large part the theme I concluded with in the last chapter—the potential of technology to help us preserve what was told. Now we end this chapter with exhilaration for the technology, but fear for how it can take issues of access out of our control and even further remove them from the narrators.

Before leaving Alaska for South Africa, I initiated a very complicated release agreement for the Kodiak Area Native Association (KANA). What made the agreement complicated was that we produced a CD-ROM with a recording of elders discussing traditional knowledge. The CD also included a recording of Aleut elders from the Aleutians. It was developed in HTML so that it could be accessed on the Internet if the communities chose to make it available that way.

In Kodiak, the people were most concerned about members of the public taking the recording and deriving income from publications. The agreement we reached permits people to use short quotes and to reference the tapes in analog form but not to reproduce large segments. The CD and Internet access remain under the control of the Kodiak and Aleut groups, who decide how they wish to distribute the program. They agreed that a copy could be available in the University of Alaska archive for use in that facility and for demonstration purposes by the staff.

The CD from Kodiak and the Aleutians has now become accessible on the Alaska Rural Systemic Initiative web site, which provides limited password access. Since the Alaska Rural Systemic Initiative funded the project and is working with the elders councils of Kodiak and the Aleutians, they should have a right to provide this type of limited access particularly because public access is already provided at Rasmuson Library for anyone who walks through the door.

We were pleasantly surprised to see this collection on a computer network because it shows that it is important enough to people for them to go to the trouble to make it available. When the Museum of the Aleutians expressed interest in having a copy, they secured permission from KANA to make it available to the public at the museum's facility in Unalaska. This was a very encouraging development because it followed the guidelines of our agreement with the Kodiak elders and further demonstrated interest in the program.

On another project, the Gates of the Arctic National Park jukebox, we were quite surprised when we heard that some of the interviews had been converted from Hypercard to a network language and posted on the Internet. We learned about this secondhand, and while we were pleased that the students who did the work cared enough about the material to transfer it to an Internet format, unsettled questions remain. The narrators may not have been consulted about this expanded exposure to their stories, although I suspect the people we interviewed are pleased that the students are providing access to their stories. Unfortunately, the students failed to credit the creators of the program. Credits are critical not only because they acknowledge creators and authors but because they let the serious scholar backtrack to the people who did the original research. And that is part of the larger process of evaluation and assessment of findings.

With wider and wider electronic access, the possibilities for distortion and misuse increase and cultural as well as personal privacy are compromised. The trade off is greater access for communities in the state. We hope that will have positive benefits of cultural and historical enrichment, but we really don't know what the negative effects will be.

At the time of this writing I have decided to take a bolder approach. We have initiated letters to all our narrators and project researchers informing them of our intention to put their recordings on the Internet. (Letters initially went to just the participants in projects that are in HTML. Additional letters will be sent to participants in our older hypercard programs at the time we transfer those programs into HTML.) Included with the letter are a copy of the narrator's signed release form and a statement of guidelines for use that users will be asked to read as part of the Internet program and that will alert users to some of the participants' concerns (see appendix C). The guidelines for use of the oral history programs refer to two documents specifically designed to help researchers working with the materials, "Guidelines for Respecting Cultural Knowledge," published by the Assembly of Alaska Native Educators for the Alaska Rural Systemic Initiative and the Standards of the Oral History Assoociation. Readers may also want to consult the "Principals for the Conduct of Research in the Arctic," (Social Science Task Force of the U.S. Interagency Arctic Research Policy Committee).

We will begin by linking our programs with local area networks such as school districts, historical and cultural societies, museums, and Native organizations. If we can successfully connect to their sites, then there is a good chance that people from the region will see and use the programs. We hope in this way to detect areas of local sensitivity. We will provide full Internet access as a second step and after local network exposure.

If a narrator objects to having their recording up on the World Wide Web, we will remove it from the site or use password access. We are, in a sense, testing the waters to see if universal electronic access will work. The benefits in terms of advancing scholarship and understanding of history and heritage could be immense. If this approach can be done in a sensitive manner, it will also make management of the recordings much easier because users will not need to come to the archive to access material.

The Western legal system is based on individual rights (see for instance, Neuenschwander 1993), but many of the cultural groups we serve have a strong concern for community rights. The impacts at that level are even harder to predict and resolve. I can envision situations where an individual would not object to his recording being on the Internet but the community might. Unfortunately, we can't predict all of the problems until we take the leap and provide wider exposure. So far, the responses have been mixed. The greatest concern comes from members of the Native community, but there are also individuals who feel that the elders wanted their stories told widely and that they should be available. So, it is hard to generalize. It should also be noted that concerns about Internet access are not limited to the Native community. For instance, the wife of a prominent figure was interviewed, and she made it clear to us that the recording is for people who come to the library. She doesn't want to focus attention on herself because she's a private person. As noted, we will be posting two documents developed by Karen Brewster: the "Use of the Project Jukebox Programs" document already mentioned and a "Site Use Agreement" (see appendix C).

The silver lining in our new initiative is the chance for increased dialogue between individuals who shared their knowledge and those of us who manage the collections. I welcome these discussions because we can learn more about issues created by greater Internet access and become more responsive to the community of people who have shared their knowledge with us. The tapes are on the shelf, the release forms filed, but there's still work to be done.

twelve

The Public Record

I first heard the hymn "Amazing Grace" over twenty years ago. I was in Beaver, Alaska, that small community on the north bank of the Yukon River that is the home of some of the people who have played such an important role in shaping my understanding of story. In that setting, the hymn came to symbolize in my mind the hard life that people were living in that place, the uncertainty of their existence, the fragility they feel, and their abiding faith in a God whose mercy they must seek in life and whose promise of comfort in death is certain. I live with a picture in my mind of a funeral in that village, a group gathered in song on a bitterly cold day. In this setting, I felt the tenuousness of life and the minute place of people in a world of natural and human disasters. I could sense the remoteness of the village, the predominant role weather played in everyone's life, and the recognition of frailty in an uncontrollable world. The people in Beaver had just witnessed murder, and I felt the inability to control violence. In this setting, I found comfort in the strong chorus of uplifted voices who believed in the abiding promise of God's care. It was their faith, not the words of the song, that lifted me up and gave me a sense of their strength amidst great sorrow.

Years later, I was shocked to hear this same song sung by a group of friends informally gathered to share their favorite folk songs. I remember thinking how out of place it seemed, how devoid of the context I knew, and, to my ears, how sacrilegious. I don't know what previous memories it held for the others, and its performance along with Negro spirituals and Irish ballads left me wondering what significance it could hold for them. Now I own a Judy Collins CD and hear her rendition of the song, so clear and perfect a production, yet so distant from my experience in Beaver. My primary association with her voice, but not the song, comes from an even earlier period of my life, before going to Alaska. That was the 1960s, which conjures up memories of college years, a time of introspection but never, for me, a time to admit our small place in the universe. I was full of hope and self-assurance, and from that period, I don't remember "Amazing Grace."

On the recommendation of a South African friend, I recently purchased a CD by the African group Ladysmith Black Mambazo. They sing a version of "Amazing Grace" arranged by Paul Simon and recorded live at the Symphony Hall in Osaka, Japan. This version is even further removed from my experience or understanding. Finally, my students pointed out to me the origin of the song: a slave trader, John Newton, repenting for his years of selling innocent people into slavery. The connotation of "wretch" took on new meaning when I read, "Until the time of his death at the age of eighty-two, John Newton never ceased to marvel at the grace of God that had transformed him so completely" (Warren 1997, 200).

In each of these diverse settings, the song speaks to different people in different ways, and there is the cumulative knowledge gleaned from each setting; yet it is the same song. The "facts" (as depicted in the words and the tune) are pretty much the same, but the setting for each performance and the background on its origin shape its meaning.

Stories on tape are like this hymn; we can listen to them and discern a message that, in a sense, stands alone, but we can go further and ask what does this particular telling mean as opposed to other tellings of the story? How is this story used by the narrator and his audience to invite, or to use Verne Harris's term again, engage meaning?

As we noted earlier, South African scholar Carolyn Hamilton (1997) points out the tension in oral documentation between those who wish to focus on story as commodity and those who see oral sources as a dynamic process by which meaning is continuously created among people. The former seeks structural understanding of stories as things with a distinct message, the latter emphasizes the fluidity of narratives, with each new setting loaded with new meaning. In the first, oral history is information, facts. In the second, it is the dynamics reflected from different tellings (Ruppert 1995; Cruikshank 1995, 1998, 25–44).

My study of stories is a bit like my experience with the hymn and a lot like Hamilton's comparison of approaches: First, I can study the story as text and attempt to generalize about what is said; for example, this is a story whose words say God is forgiving and is our hope. Second, I can attempt to find what is common in all contexts, in other words, attempt to determine the bounds of the story; for example, this is always a story sung reverently, although we recognize that reverence and its expression can take many forms. Third, I can take a more fluid approach and explore how the story expands as different people use it to impart their meaning. Following the last approach, I look for differences as well as similarities and see both as contributors to my understanding of the story. (How much richer my understanding is after hearing the story of the slave trader). While I am clearly an advocate of an inclusive approach because it gives us a fuller understanding of stories' content, I also think it more clearly reflects the multiple ways people use stories to convey meaning.

Such inclusiveness does raise challenges for a curator of collections though. The approach advocated here transforms the curator from a caretaker to a creator of records, a person whose mark on the record is visible to all. Terry Cook, formerly of the National Archives of Canada, in his opening remarks to a group of African archivists, said, "archivists will continue to shift their research emphasis from the analysis of the properties and characteristics of individual documents, to an analysis of the functions, processes, and transactions which cause documents to be created" (Cook 1997, 21). At that same meeting, Verne Harris concluded his remarks with, "Our realities demand that we see ourselves preeminently as thinkers and shapers; they demand that we learn to become movers and shakers" (Harris 1997b, 70).

Both men recognize that future users of collections will want as much information about each recording as possible, and they will want to know who created the record and how they did it. As Trouillot says, "Archives assemble. Their assembly work is not limited to a more or less passive act of collecting. Rather, it is an active act of production that prepares facts for historical intelligibility. Archives set up both the substantive and formal elements of the narrative. They are the institutionalized sites of mediation between the sociohistorical process and the narrative about that process" (Trouillot 1995, 52).

Review of Necessary Supporting Documentation

A great deal can be done to prepare the record for future researchers without infringing on the researchers' role to interpret according to their understanding of the subject, the narrator, and the particular setting. Categories of information an archive should provide include ethical and legal concerns, such as the conditions under which the recording can be used and the concerns of the individual and their community (see chapter 10). Commonly, this includes comments about media representation or Internet access (see chapter 9). Next is the issue of interpretation. In order to ensure the best possibility for accurate interpretation, it is helpful to cross-reference to other materials that address the topics discussed, with special reference to variants of a story and different cultural interpretations. An as complete as possible description of setting and context will help future researchers in their analysis. Supporting documentation should also indicate why this recording is a part of the archive and why it was selected. This consideration forces the curator to think about the recording in light of his or her role in the shaping of a historical record, as opposed to seeing himself as a passive recipient of material. All this implies that the curator shapes the emerging record.

To do this well, one has to know the outlines of the history documented by recordings and the backgrounds of the people who tell the stories. I take this a step further and try to identify with the messages implicit in each telling. That implies not only an acceptance and reliance on story in my own life but also a very conscious recognition and explanation of how I am part of and influenced by what Verne terms the "terrain of social memory" (Harris 1996, 7).

I believe that we need to see a good distance over the terrain of social memory and recognize how particular locales within it fit into a total setting. That demands personal recognition of, and identification with, the terrain as it exists in stories people have told, of the ways they use story to shape new contours in the terrain, and of our role in supporting the ever-emerging new forms. And to go one step further, I think we need to create settings where cross-fertilization of knowledge can occur.

"Production of History"

David Cohen challenges us to see history as a continuous process of formulating and looking for different ways people express their understandings (1994, 244). If Cohen is right, then how can we be sure the recordings that line the shelves of the archive will be part of this process? How can they be available in ways that invite promotion of multi-faceted historical analysis by a wide-ranging audience— from the Native elder to the university scholar? In what new settings could the recordings appear? I suggest we haven't thought deeply enough about who our audiences are and what their interests might be. It is simply not good enough to answer that our audiences are those who make their way through our archival doors. We have to, as Verne would say, cultivate users.

There is a certain irony that the recordings in our archives at UAF are used by students and a few scholars but are rarely referenced or used by elders or other members of the Native communities where they originated. Part of the reason collections aren't used more is that the oral history is pale compared to talk with a fellow elder or even one's memory of the elder telling a story. The oral history tape is only a reminder of a performance, an occasion that was charged with the interplay of personalities, intent, and setting.

The challenge is to figure out how the recording can continue to inform and stimulate discussions of history and culture. In short, it must be reset into a context of discussion; it must be interpreted and represented; it must be united with people's experience and imagination in much the same way as writing provides a completion and connection over time (Sarris 1993, 38). We can do this by the way we represent recordings to the public in exhibits, radio, television, and interactive computer-based programs that link the recordings to photos, maps, and text. And we can do it in public performances of story.[30]

Each of these formats extends the visibility of recordings and helps give the cues necessary to contextualize them (Bauman and Briggs 1990, 69) in their present application. One of the things we have learned from the oral tradition is that stories need to be retold, reapplied over and over, so their meaning can extend and nourish our understanding of the world. In each case, the goal is to get people to think and talk about what was shared in the storytelling and not to view the original telling as the final statement. That's why I was so excited to hear about the use of Ch'eghwetsen' to promote a program for children and to learn that the program is run by the Fairbanks Native Association (Tarnai 2001). I think this interpretation and representation of the concept would particularly please Peter John.

What is proposed here is active participation in the process of reintroducing oral recordings in places where people will talk about them and extend the story into new settings. The process brings the static record a step closer to the oral tradition by reinvigorating both the record and the tradition with new discussion. This is not going to be easy, but it could expand and reinform what is now a rather narrow record. To the extent we have the resources and will to keep the dialogue open, the record will evolve in ever more meaningful ways. We surely will find many new situations to confront, and the negotiation of meaning and use (representation) will evolve in ways we can't at present imagine.

The potential of oral history lies not just in what is on the tape but in how people connect that information to their understanding of the past and present. The curator has the pleasant responsibility of imagining these connections and preserving a record that expands, as opposed to constricts, meaning.[31] I had an example of this last winter. On our local public broadcasting station, Randy Accord, an aviator and keen observer of Alaskan aviation history, was interviewed about the crash of Will Rogers and Wiley Post at the site of Walakpa (Ualiqpaat) near Barrow, back in 1935. Randy went into great detail about the reasons the plane went down and how it could have been prevented. When he got to how the people in Barrow knew about the crash, he mentioned that there were Eskimos camped at the site and one of them ran to Barrow with the tragic news.

That's about the extent of what Randy told, but I knew there was much more to the story. The heroic effort to fly the bodies out of Barrow attracted national attention (Potter 1973, 86–88). I also knew that the site of the crash was an important Native summer and fall camp and an ancient archeological site (Stanford 1976; Schneider, Pedersen, and Libbey 1980, 187–96). I vaguely remembered that Sadie Brower Neakok had told Margay Blackman about the crash in one of the interviews for her life history (Blackman 1989). Excited about this prospect of rediscovering a local perspective on the event, I dug up the transcripts of Margay's interviews and found the section where Sadie talked about the crash:

> There was a time . . . you know, today it's a Memorial Day for Will Rogers and Wiley Post up here; because that's the day we were getting ready to . . . August . . . I was getting all these kids ready to go out on the *North Star*[32] . . . and writing to them and writing back. We had no planes then. We'd heard, after Dad's trip down there . . . he knew Will Rogers quite well . . . and he was going to try to get his old friend from Oklahoma, Wiley Post, interested in flying him up here that spring, which never happened . . .
>
> We heard the plane, but there was families still out camping who'd been seal hunting with their boats out there in that Walakpa area . . . Like Bert Okakok's family, Claire Okpeaha's family, and

there were two others. . . . They said there was a little opening in the sky, clear, and Wiley Post saw it and then he came down, landed in that cove, that water, which wasn't too deep. And they got out of the plane, and talked to these people. They were the only people that these two saw there at that camp. Claire Okpeaha, after their plane took off, said it went . . . about 65 feet and just nosedived into that shallow area . . .

So this man Claire ran all the way from that distance. And when he reached the hospital, he collapsed from exhaustion. He had to be treated . . . And it shook us so bad, and scared us so bad, that no one ever wanted to go on a plane after that. When we finally, in September, the first week in September . . . these kids that were interested in school . . . I left Barrow in 1935 . . . After this crash had happened. When we got into Kotzebue, the kids were scared to get on the plane. (Recording by Margaret Blackman of Sadie Brower Neakok, August 15, 1984, Tape 1, side 2)

What began as a Will Rogers and Wiley Post story turns out to also be a story about what it was like for students to go out for schooling and their first experiences on airplanes. In Sadie's account, we can clearly imagine how difficult it was for those students to get on an airplane after the crash, and that adds a new dimension to the Will Rogers and Wiley Post story, to hear how the crash affected the students.

Imagine my surprise last January when I heard on the radio an interview that concerned the event, this time with June Hall, curator of a quilt exhibit that was traveling to the University of Alaska Museum. She told the story of the Morgan quilt. This quilt was made by Moe Post, the mother of Wiley Post, and presented to Stanley Morgan and his family. Stanley was the radio operator in Barrow and had been instrumental in the communication about the disaster and the retrieval of the bodies (Harris 2001, 36–37). Now, this quilt is another part of the story—this time the relationship between a grieving mother and a family living in the distant and remote place where her son died.

The fun in oral history comes when we see the multitude of new directions that a story takes and when we present them side by side. When we are really doing our job, we can't stand to see the stories sit quietly on the shelves; we welcome the invitation to discuss, elaborate, and make connections to other sources. That's our privilege and our job.

Appendix
Oral History Gift and Release Agreement

Thank you for your generous contribution of knowledge to the Oral History Archives. We welcome the opportunity to have the (audio or video) recording made with you on _____. The Oral History Archives agrees to preserve your recording and make it available to the public.

In consideration of the role of the Archives in preserving and making your recording available, we ask you to agree to the following:

I, _____, transfer to the University of Alaska Fairbanks' Rasmuson Library my title, interest, and copyright to the recording.

I also agree not to hold the University of Alaska Fairbanks liable for how it makes the recordings available and how it preserves them. I further acknowledge that I have been informed of the following:

- The Oral History Program makes recordings available to researchers, writers, scholars, students, and the interested public.

- The Library may make this recording electronically accessible via local area networks, the Internet, or other electronic means for access and preservation purposes.

- While the Library only intends to make the recordings available for educational and/or non-commercial purposes, by signing this form I release the Library and the University from liability in cases where individuals who access a recording might violate these conditions.

Please be assured that we will do all that we can to inform users of these conditions and thereby minimize the potential for misuse. **None of the above mentioned conditions restricts you from re-telling and/or recording again any of the information you gave on this recording.**

_____   _____
(Narrator's printed name)   (Date)

_____
(Narrator's printed mailing address)

_____
(Narrator's signature)

_____   _____
(Interviewer's printed name & signature)   (Date)

_____
(Collection manager's signature)

Appendix B
Interview Restrictions

Interviews accepted into the University of Alaska Fairbanks Oral History Collection *must be available* for public use. We cannot accept recordings where:

1 **The narrator or other body must be consulted prior to each use of the interview.** Such a restriction severely reduces the circulation and usefulness of the tape and makes long term management impossible.

2 **Individuals and/or members of particular groups are forbidden to use the interview.** Both the UAF Oral History Program and the Rasmuson Library are firmly committed to the principles of intellectual freedom and will not accept any form of discrimination.

3 **The interviewer and/or narrator prohibits the UAF Oral History Program from making copies of the interviews and/or insists upon retaining the right to sell copies.** We need to be able to make copies of interviews for circulation, preservation, transcription purposes and for the narrators and their families.

We do allow some *limited restrictions* to be placed on certain interviews under the following circumstances:

1 Interviews to be used in a book or other publication project can be restricted from public use for *no more than two years*. At the end of two years, the tapes will be made available to the public regardless of whether or not anything has been published.

2 Officials can restrict public access to their own interviews until they leave public office provided that they will be leaving office in *two years or less*. At the end of two years, the tape will be made available to the public regardless of whether or not they have left office.

3 Radio programs typically retain rebroadcast rights to interviews that they have produced unless they choose to relinquish that right to the UAF Oral History Program.

The Oral History Program requires that you observe the following guidelines if you wish to place a recording in the Oral History Collection:

1 All recordings received at the Oral History Program *must* have a UAF Release Form, signed by the interviewee, on file at the Oral History Program office within four (4) weeks of receipt of the recording by the Oral History Program.

2 Interviews *cannot* be restricted beyond the life span of the A/V medium. For example, it is pointless to restrict a tape for 100 years if the recording only has a shelf life of 10 years.

3 The UAF Oral History Program *does not* warehouse collections. Anyone seeking to have their tapes restricted from public use and stored for a period of time should consult commercial vendors who specialize in this service.

4 If copies of interviews are to be deposited with several institutions, *all* of the institutions should be named in the release form. If UAF is one of the named institutions, it should be *noted in the release* that we make our collections available to the public.

Appendix
Internet Use of Oral History Programs

Use of the Project Jukebox Programs

The University of Alaska Fairbanks Oral History Program holds copyright to the recordings and transcripts and provides access to these materials strictly for educational and research purposes. The fact that recordings and transcripts are posted on this site provides public access to them but does not constitute a right to copy and/or publish these oral history materials. No use (beyond limited quotation) should be made of these interviews without the express permission of the UAF Oral History Program. Permission must be obtained for publication of any material beyond that which might jeopardize the integrity or value of the whole copyrighted work, as covered in the Fair Use portion of United States copyright law. To gain permission write Dr. William Schneider, Oral History Curator at ffwss@uaf.edu or UAF Oral History Program, Elmer E. Rasmuson Library, UAF, Fairbanks, AK 99775.

We ask that researchers approach the material with respect for, and awareness of, the cultures and individuals whose lives, ideas, and creativity are represented here. Because of the dangers of cross-cultural misunderstandings we encourage users to become knowledgeable in the cultural backgrounds of the speakers before interpreting and referencing these works in print or media publications. Users are strongly encouraged to consult the Guidelines for Respecting Cultural Knowledge established by the Assembly of Alaska Native Educators at **http://www.ankn.uaf.edu/standards/culturaldoc.html**, and the Principles and Standards of the Oral History Association at **http://www.dickinson.edu/organizations/oha/EvaluationGuidelines.html**.

UAF Homepage Oral History Database Projects
Button Button Button
(goes to Site Use Agreement)

Site Use Agreement

As a user of this site, you agree to:

1) Not use the material for commercial purposes. Short quotes and references are permitted for instructional and publication purposes.

2) Provide complete citations referencing speaker, interviewer, date, tape
number, jukebox program, and Website with URL Address.

3) Not re-post or link this site or any parts of it to another program or listing.

4) Follow the *Guidelines for Respecting Cultural Knowledge* and the *Principles
and Standards of the Oral History Association.*

Unauthorized attempts to upload information or change information on
this site are strictly prohibited and may be punishable under the Computer
Fraud and Abuse Act of 1986 and the National Information Infrastructure
Protection Act of 1995.

For site security purposes and to ensure that this service remains available
to all users, this computer system employs software programs to monitor
network traffic to identify unauthorized attempts to upload or change information, or otherwise cause damage. No other attempts are made to identify
individual users or their usage habits.

AGREE BUTTON DO NOT AGREE BUTTON
(TAKES YOU INTO SITE) (BACK TO USE OF PROGRAMS PAGE)

Notes

1. Sentsho Ernest Mphahlele, a graduate of the University of the North, has written about the establishment of universities specifically for non-Whites in South Africa. He notes that the University of Durbin in Westville was established for Indians, the University of the Western Cape for Coloreds (people of mixed ancestry), and three universities—Fort Hare, the University of Zululand, and the University of the North—for Africans. The University of the North was established specifically for the cultural groups in the Northern Province. Students began classes in January 1960 (Mphahele 1992, 1, 35). The University of the North (UNIN) is located about a half hour drive north of Pietersburg in a place that was specially named "Sovenga," a new term to signify the Northern Sotho, Venda, and Tswana peoples who were to attend the school.

2. I discussed this speech during a presentation at the University of Witwatersrand and was pleased to get comments from experts in African oral narrative. An abstract of my comments was published in volume 40 of the *South African Archives Journal* (1998), under the title "More Than Words on a Tape: The Problematic in Converting Orality to Material Custody" (Schneider 1998a, 94–100).

3. My colleague David Krupa uses the term to describe Chief Peter John (Krupa 1999), and he has led me to Renato Rosaldo, who uses the term in his foreword to Garcia Canclini's book *Hybrid Cultures: Strategies for Entering and Leaving Modernity*. There *transculturation* describes the continuous "two way borrowing and lending between cultures" (xv). My use of the term follows from Krupa and Rosaldo and recognizes the significance of modernity and access to worldwide influences, but my focus is on the individual and on the dynamics of choice in shaping identity. Again David led me, this time to Clifford Geertz, who emphasizes the role of individuals who create useful structures and institutions to meet their interests and needs. Geertz states, "Believing with Max Weber that man is an animal suspended in webs of significance he himself has spun, I take culture to be those webs and the analysis of it to be therefore not an experimental science in search of law but an interpretive one in search of meaning" (1973, 5).

4. Frederica de Laguna may have grown up and spent much of her academic career at Bryn Mawr, but she was also a seasoned traveler in the North. In 1935, she organized an archaeological survey of the lower

Tanana and middle and lower Yukon. They built their own boats and left from Nenana (de Laguna 1947, 1995).

5. Grant Spearman points out this may be located at the mouth of the Itkillik River, where it joins the Colville River. See Hoffman, Libbey, and Spearman, n.d., 167–89.

6. Fortunately, many of Johnny and Sarah Frank's stories have been preserved and are now in print. They were compiled and edited by Craig Mishler (1995).

7. When I told this story to colleagues at Laval University, they wondered whether the old woman had an established relationship with Waldo before his first kill. Perhaps she was the midwife who delivered him or they shared the same name. I wish now that I had asked!

8. When we first demonstrated the jukebox program, it was at the national Oral History Association meeting in Salt Lake City (Snowbird) in 1991. At that time there were only a few programs in the country doing similar projects. The Library of Congress had one called American Memory. Now, electronic delivery of oral history has become very popular. We are still one of the few programs that presents a large number of full-length recordings in an electronically retrievable format. We do this because we want users to be able to access the whole recording, not just the sections we think are most important. My colleague Karen Brewster has produced a useful survey of other programs and how they are dealing with ethical issues of electronic delivery (see www.uaf.edu/library/collections/apr/internet.oralhist/).

9. In her book on the community of Milton Keynes, Ruth Finnegan has a subsection of a chapter that also bears the title "What's in a Story." She succinctly and eloquently describes the four main attributes of stories: (1) they have a sense of direction either in terms of temporal or sequential framing of an event, occurrence, or person; (2) they help explain or bring coherence to a subject; (3) the themes or events described have the potential to be generalized to other events, settings, or issues; and (4) the accounts are presented within a framework that is familiar to an audience; there's a degree of what she would term "shared expectations" (Finnegan 1998, 9–14).

10. The Truth and Reconciliation hearings were established to publicly air the atrocities that had been committed and to provide a way for some resolution in the future. The hearings are discussed in detail in chapter 6.

11. The Communities of Memory Project, sponsored by the Alaska Humanities Forum, created public forums around Alaska to tell stories about life in the communities and to enhance understanding between community members as they explored through story their personal and collective experiences. Sessions were held in Unalaska, Nome, Kotzebue, Fairbanks, Wasilla, Anchorage, Juneau, Kenai, Homer, and Bethel.

12. Alan Lomax's work has been a rich source of information on the background of popular folk songs (Lomax 1975).

13. For a brief history of the Hitchcock Chair factory in Connecticut, see Moore 1933. See also Kenney 1971.

14. Dell Hymes has been a leader in demonstrating how to work with oral narrative to uncover the structures of meaning, in his terms, "the underlying rules and regularities which make performances possible and intelligible" (1981, 79). Dennis Tedlock has pioneered methods of reproducing oral narrative in text form in order to preserve the way the story is told and the context of the telling, as well as the text of the narration. He writes, "The trick worth learning, I think, is to tell the story of what performers have said and done while at the same time letting their performances go on telling a story, and to do this not by separating voices *between* different passages or sequences but by letting different voices be heard *within* each passage or segment" (Tedlock 1990, 141).

15. For purposes of emphasis, I quote Tishu as I heard her tell the story. Because I recall the way she told the story so clearly, I think an ethnopoetic transcription helps to convey what she emphasized. I don't usually feel comfortable using this format for retellings, in part because I don't trust my reconstructions of the cadence and emphasis. In this case, perhaps because of the deliberateness of her storytelling, I felt I could do it. This is the way I originally reported the story (1995b, 80).

16. This example is a very oversimplified picture of Inupiaq perceptions, and we must remind ourselves that there are differences of opinion between individuals and between communities over onshore versus offshore oil development. The interviews were done in the early 1980s, and times have changed.

17. Both acts involved decisions about new ownership and new management schemes for the land. ANCSA created private lands for Native groups, while ANILCA determined management on large tracts of public land. In each case, the traditional Native patterns of land use and occupancy now have to operate under new laws with new restrictions. The Native regional and village corporations established under ANCSA provide new opportunities within non-Native, or Western, commercial and legal spheres, but the map of Alaska has become a patchwork of ownership patterns reflecting different management regimes. That is the present climate, far different from what those early Tanana chiefs sought, although they predicted that changes to their way of life were inevitable.

18. The Alaska Native Review Commission hearings were conducted by Chief Justice Thomas Berger and were modeled after the hearing process he conducted in the Yukon and Northwest Territories to assess the impact of the proposed Mackenzie Valley Pipeline. In that inquiry, thirty-five communities were visited to elicit comments on the proposed action (Berger 1977).

19. This quote is by Phyllis Morrow and is taken from the conclusion of a book of essays on the Communities of Memory Project (Morrow n.d., 2)

20. In the post-apartheid government, where elections are held and the government is democratic, the chief's authority comes into question. The Department of Provincial and Local Government, Directorate of Traditional Affairs has produced a white paper on this subject, "White

Paper on Traditional Leadership," although I do not know if formal, legislative action has been taken.

21. Similar examples of collaborative research are presented by Larry Evers and Barre Toelken (2001).

22. Es'kia Mphahlele wrote about this experience in his autobiography (1984).

23. Charles Briggs has written about the interview context and provides useful discussion about the multiple factors that influence communication in the cross-cultural context. He would add to my minimal list: message form, reference, channel, code, social roles, interactional goals, social situation, and type of communicative event (Briggs 1986, 100–101).

24. *Oral biography* is the term I use to title a publication series at the University of Alaska Press. The series features first-person life histories based on oral recordings, with commentary and contextual statements provided by a separate author. That author determines, in consultation with the narrator, the way the written text will be organized and presented. Some people find oral biography to be a misleading and contradictory category because oral in this context reflects authorship by the narrator and subject, while biography means somebody writing about another person's life. I continue to use the term oral biography because the works entail tension between oral memoir (first-person spoken autobiography) and an author's representation of that narrative in written form for a reading audience. The tension is inherent in this genre of life history, and the title helps the reader become aware of it.

25. Chase develops this theme in his book on the language of subsistence in the Bethel area, *Telling Our Selves: Ethnicity and Discourse in Southwestern Alaska* (1996).

25. But the last word, for the moment, rests with Chief Peter John. He gave a recording of the "Blind Man and the Loon" that is by far the most interesting and extensive in detail. This recording was made with Jim Kari and Jeff Leer of the Alaska Native Language Center, University of Alaska Fairbanks, tape number ANLC 2522.

27. Dan is fond of quoting Gary Trudeau's 1987 address to the Smith College graduates: "The impertinent question is the glory and the engine of human inquiry . . . Copernicus asked it and shook the foundations of Renaissance Europe. Darwin asked it and is repudiated to this day. Thomas Jefferson asked it and was so invigorated by it that he declared it an inalienable right . . . History's movers framed their questions in ways that were entirely disrespectful of conventional wisdom" (Trudeau 1987, 4–8).

28. This is not the case everywhere. In Canada, "public archives" hold collections of oral history that may have restricted access controlled by particular First Nations. The Yukon Archives in Whitehorse, for instance, is obligated under land claims legislation to hold and preserve First Nations recordings, regardless of whether they are accessible to all potential users.

29. Ironically, there is a children's rhyme about Makgoba's death by beheading, but I am told that it is not sung in a disrespectful manner.

30. This last point was reinforced in my mind at a meeting in Dawson of scientists, park managers, cultural specialists, and First Nation elders. Louise Proffit LeBlanc used this setting to talk about the "Traveler Stories." Traveler is a mythological figure who created the Athabascan world and established order. Louise's choice of these stories was particularly appropriate because the stories are told on both sides of the border between Canada and the United States and because this creator traveled the river as he established the order we are meant to recognize. She reminded us of this common heritage and why it is important today. At this meeting we heard scientists talk about the geology and the prehistoric fauna. It was very fitting that Louise would remind us of this ancient mythological tie and to suggest that Traveler and his wisdom still lives for her and that his story has a place at this conference. Louise knew just how to bring the old stories into new light (Upper Yukon River Region Heritage Symposium, March 8–10, 2001).

31. Sello Hatang makes a similar point in a discussion with Verne Harris (Harris and Hatang 2000, 57).

32. This was the Bureau of Indian Affairs supply ship that came north each year to bring goods to the communities, provide basic medical care, and transport officials and students leaving for school.

References

African Wisdom Creations. 2000. The African Renaissance Deck.

Ager, Lynn P. (Wallen). 1971. "The Eskimo Storyknife Complex of Southwestern Alaska." Master's thesis, Department of Anthropology, University of Alaska Fairbanks.

Alaska Library Association. 1974. Songs and Legends Oral History Collection. Copies of the collection at the Alaska and Polar Regions Department, Elmer Rasmuson Library, University of Alaska Fairbanks.

Alaska Rural Systemic Initiative. 2000. "Guidelines for Respecting Cultural Knowledge." *Sharing Our Pathways* (newsletter of the Alaska Rural Systemic Initiative) 5 (March/April).

Alaska State Library. Kayamorri Photo Collection, Historical Collections, Juneau.

Allen, Barbara. 1988. "Oral History: The Folk Connection." Pp. 15–26 in *The Past Meets the Present: Essays on Oral History*, eds. David Stricklin and Rebecca Sharpless. Lanham, Maryland: University Press of America.

Allen, Barbara, and Lynwood Montell. 1981. *From Memory to History, Using Oral Sources in Local Historical Research.* Nashville: The American Association for State and Local History.

Amadi, Adolphe O. 1981. *African Libraries: Western Tradition and Colonial Brainwashing.* New Jersey: Scarecrow Press.

Anderson, Jean. 1999. "Secondhand Talk: 'Voice' in the Evolving Literature of Alaska." Paper delivered at the national Oral History Association meetings, Anchorage, Alaska.

Arnaktauyok, Germaine. 1998. "Germaine Arnaktauyok." Exhibit, Winnipeg Art Gallery, Arts Induvik Canada Inc., 1 February–6 September.

Arnold, Robert. 1976. *Alaska Native Land Claims.* Anchorage: Alaska Native Foundation.

Arundale, Wendy, and Eliza Jones. 1989. "Historic Land Use Processes in Alaska's Koyukuk River Area." *Arctic* 42 (2): 148–62.

Basso, Keith. 1996. *Wisdom Sits in Places: Landscape and Language Among the Western Apache.* Albuquerque: University of New Mexico Press.

Battle, M. 1995. "The Ubuntu Theology of Desmond Tutu: How Desmond Tutu's Theological Model of Community Facilitates Reconciliation among Races in a System of Apartheid." Ph.D. dissertation, Department of Religion, Duke University.

Bauman, Richard. 1986. *Story, Performance, and Event, Contextual Studies of Oral Narrative.* Cambridge. Cambridge University Press.

Bauman, Richard, and Charles L. Briggs. 1990. "Poetics and Performance as Critical Perspectives on Language and Social Life." *Annual Review of Anthropology* 19: 59–88.
Behar, Ruth. 1993. *Translated Woman: Crossing the Border with Esperanza's Story.* Boston: Beacon Press.
Berger, Thomas R. 1977. *Northern Frontier, Northern Homeland: The Report of the Mackenzie Valley Pipeline Inquiry.* Toronto: James Lorimer and Co.
Berry, Mary Clay. 1975. *The Alaska Pipeline: The Politics of Oil and Native Land Claims.* Bloomington: Indiana University Press.
Blackman, Margaret. 1982 and 1992. *During My Time: Florence Edenshaw Davidson, a Haida Woman.* Seattle: University of Washington Press.
———. 1989. *Sadie Brower Neakok, an Inupiaq Woman.* Seattle: University of Washington Press.
Blowsnake, Sam. 1983. *Crashing Thunder: The Autobiography of an American Indian.* Edited by Paul Radin. Lincoln: University of Nebraska Press; originally published, New York: D. Appleton, 1926.
Bockstoce, John R. 1995. *Whales, Ice, and Men: The History of Whaling in the Western Arctic.* Seattle: University of Washington Press in association with the New Bedford Whaling Museum.
Bodfish, Waldo. 1991. *Kusiq: An Eskimo Life History from the Arctic Coast of Alaska.* Edited by William Schneider. Fairbanks: University of Alaska Press.
Bozzoli, Belinda. 1991. *Women of Phokeng: Consciousness, Life Strategy, and Migrancy in South Africa, 1900–1983.* Portsmouth: Heinemann.
Brewster, Karen. 1998. "An Umialik's Life: Conversations with Harry Brower Sr." Manuscript. Rasmuson Library, University of Alaska Fairbanks.
Briggs, Charles. 1986. *Learning How to Ask: A Sociolinguistic Appraisal of the Value of the Interview in Social Science Research.* Cambridge: Cambridge University Press.
Burch, Ernest. 1971. "The Non-Empirical Environment of the Arctic Alaskan Eskimos." *Southwestern Journal of Anthropology* 27 (2): 148–65.
———. 1986. *The Inupiaq Eskimo Nations of Northwest Alaska.* Fairbanks: University of Alaska Press.
Bureau of Indian Affairs. 1995. BIA ANCSA: Nunivak Overview, BLM AA-9238 et al., Calista Corporation. Vol. 2, "Site Abstracts", p. 32.
Carroll, James A. 1957. *The First Ten Years in Alaska: Memoirs of a Fort Yukon Trapper, 1911–1922.* New York: Exposition Press.
Clark, Annette McFadyen. 1974. *Koyukuk River Culture.* Mercury Series, Canadian Ethnology Service Paper 18. Ottawa: National Museum of Man.
Cohen, David. 1994. *The Combing of History.* Chicago: University of Chicago Press.
Cook, Terry. 1997. "The Place of Archives and Archives as Place: Preserving Societal Memory at the End of the Millennium." Pp. 12–24 in *The Nature, Identity, and Role of Public Archives in Southern and Eastern Africa at the End of the Twentieth Century.* Proceedings of the Fourteenth Biennial General Conference of the Eastern and Southern Africa Regional Branch of the International Council on Archives, Pretoria, 30 July–1 August.
Cruikshank, Julie. 1990. *Life Lived Like a Story: Life Stories of Three Yukon Native Elders,* Lincoln: University of Nebraska Press.

―――. 1991. *Dän Dháts'edenintth'é: Reading Voices, Oral and Written Interpretations of the Yukon's Past.* Vancouver: Douglas and McIntyre.

―――. 1995. "'Pete's Song': Establishing Meanings through Story and Song." In collaboration with Angela Sidney. Pp. 53–75 in *When Our Words Return: Writing, Hearing, and Remembering Oral Traditions of Alaska and the Yukon.* Edited by Phyllis Morrow and William Schneider. Logan: Utah State University Press.

―――. 1998. *The Social Life of Stories: Narrative and Knowledge in the Yukon Territory.* Lincoln: University of Nebraska Press.

Cruikshank, Moses. 1986. *The Life I've Been Living,* Fairbanks: University of Alaska Press.

Dauenhauer, Nora Marks, and Richard Dauenhauer. 1987. *Haa Shuká, Our Ancestors: Tlingit Oral Narratives.* Seattle: University of Washington Press.

Davis, Nancy Yaw. 1971. "The Effects of the 1964 Alaska Earthquake, Tsunami, and Resettlement on Two Koniag Eskimo Villages." Ph.D. dissertation, Department of Anthropology, University of Washington.

De Laguna, Frederica. 1947. *The Prehistory of North America as Seen from the Yukon.* Memoirs of the Society for American Archaeology, no. 3. Menasha, Wisconsin.

―――. 1995. *Tales from the Dena, Indian Stories from the Tanana, Koyukuk and Yukon Rivers.* Seattle: University of Washington Press.

Drozda, Robert. 1995. "'They Talked of the Land with Respect': Interethnic Communication in the Documentation of Historical Places and Cemetery Sites." Pp. 99–122 in *When Our Words Return: Writing, Hearing, and Remembering Oral Traditions of Alaska and the Yukon.* Edited by Phyllis Morrow and William Schneider. Logan: Utah State University Press.

Drozda, Robert, and Howard T. Amos. 1997. "Qikertamteni Nunat Atrit Nuniwarmiuni: The Names of Places on Our Island, Nunivak." Unpublished manuscript.

Dunaway, David. 1991. "The Oral Biography." *Biography* 14(3):256–66

Evers, Larry and Barre Toelken. 2001. *Native American Oral Traditions, Collaboration and Interpretation.* Logan, Utah State University Press.

Fairbanks Daily News-Miner. 1915. "The Natives Ask for Schools and Land," 7 July, p. 3.

―――. 1999. "Egypt blasts U.S. Officials for Suspecting Backup Pilot." *New York Times* article in the *News-Miner,* 18 November, A1 & A7, p. 58.

―――. 2000. "Ring Links Deceased Dad with Daughter." Associated Press article, 4 February, A1 & A7.

―――. 2000. "Plane Crash Victim's Ring Returned to Daughter," Associated Press article, 6 February, p. 58.

Felipowicz, Eugene. 1999. Slide-tape, Oral History Research Project on icons, prepared for anthropology class, Oral Sources, p. 56.

Finnegan, Ruth. 1970. *Oral Literature in Africa.* Nairobi: Oxford University Press.

―――. 1992. *Oral Traditions and the Verbal Arts.* London: Routledge.

―――. 1998. *Tales of the City: A Study of Narrative and Urban Life.* Cambridge: Cambridge University Press.

Foley, John Miles. 1995. *The Singer of Tales in Performance.* Bloomington: Indiana University Press.

Frisch, Michael. 1989. *A Shared Authority*. State University of New York Series in Oral and Public History. Albany: State University of New York Press.

Geertz, Clifford. 1973. *The Interpretation of Cultures*. New York: Basic Books.

Giddings, Louis. 1961. *Kobuk River People*. Studies of Northern Peoples 1, Fairbanks: Department of Anthropology and Geography. University of Alaska Fairbanks.

Glassie, Henry. 1982. *Passing the Time in Ballymenone*. Bloomington: Indiana University Press.

Glatthorn, Barbara. 1997. "Life History." Manuscript on Dorothea Leighton, in possession of William Schneider, University of Alaska Fairbanks.

Gluck, Sherna. 1987. *Rosie the Riveter Revisited*. New York: Penguin.

Gmelch, Sharon. 1986. *Nan: The Life of an Irish Travelling Woman*. New York: Norton.

Haley, Alex. 1976. *Roots*. Garden City: Doubleday.

Hall, Edwin. 1998 (1975). *The Eskimo Storyteller: Folktales from Noatak, Alaska*. Fairbanks: University of Alaska Press.

Hamilton, Carolyn. 1997. "Living by Fluidity: Oral Histories, Material Custodies and the Politics of Preservation." Paper presented at the international conference, Words and Voices: Critical Practices of Orality in Africa and African Studies. Bellagio Study and Conference Centre, Italy, 24–28 February.

———. 1998. *Terrific Majesty: The Power of Shaka Zulu and the Limits of Historical Invention*. Cambridge: Harvard University Press.

Hansen, Susan. n.d. "Village Notes," Cooperative Park Studies Unit, Alaska Native Claims Settlement Act 14(h)1 Collection.

Harrington, Rebie. 1937. *Cinderella Takes a Holiday in the Northland*. New York: Fleming H. Revell.

Harris, Alma. 2001. *Quilts of Alaska, A Textile Album of the Last Frontier*. Juneau: Gasteneau Historical Society.

Harris, Verne. 1996. "Redefining Archives in South Africa: Public Archives and Society in Transition, 1990–1996." *Archivaria: The Journal of the Association of Canadian Archivists* 42 (fall): 6–27.

———. 1997a. "Claiming Less, Delivering More: A Critique of Positivist Formulations on Archives in South Africa." Paper presented at the seminar, The Role Records Play in Revealing the Past. University of Natal, Pietermaritzburg. Published in *Archivaria* 44 (1997): 132–141.

———. 1997b. "Probing Pattern in the Institutional Landscape of Archives." Pp. 67–71 in *The Nature, Identity, and Role of Public Archives in Southern and Eastern Africa at the End of the Twentieth Century*. Proceedings of the Fourteenth Biennial General Conference of the Eastern and Southern Africa Regional Branch of the International Council on Archives, Pretoria, 30 July–1 August.

Harris, Verne. and Sello Hatang. 2000. "Archives Identity and Place: A Dialogue on What It (Might) Mean(s) To Be an African Archivist." *ESARBICA* 19: 45–58.

Hatang, Sello. 2000. "Converting Orality to Material Culture: Is It a Noble Act of Liberation or Is It an Act of Incarceration?" *ESARBICA* 19: 22–30.

Hensel, Chase. 1996. *Telling Our Selves: Ethnicity and Discourse in Southwestern Alaska*. New York: Oxford University Press.

Herbert, Belle. 1982. *Shandaa: In My Lifetime.* Told by Belle Herbert, recorded and edited by Bill Pfisterer with assistance of Alice Moses, transcribed and translated by Katherine Peter, edited by Jane McGary. Fairbanks: Alaska Native Language Center.

Hinckley, Ted C. 1970. "The Canoe Rocks: We Do Not Know What Will Become of Us." *Western Historical Quarterly* 1 (3): 265–90.

Hoffman, David, David Libbey, and Grant Spearman. n.d. *Nuiqsut, A Study of Land Use Values Through Time.* Fairbanks and Barrow: Cooperative Park Studies Unit and the North Slope Borough.

Hofmeyr, Isabel. 1993. *We Spend Our Years as a Tale That Is Told.* Portsmouth: Heinemann.

Housing Central Executive Committee. 1993. "Background to the Renaming Campaign and Brief Explanation Around the Names of Our Residence." Tommy Ntsewa, Chairperson, University of the North, Sovenga, November.

Hughes, Charles. 1974. *Eskimo Boyhood: An Autobiography in Psychological Perspective.* Lexington: The University Press of Kentucky.

Hymes, Dell. 1981. *In Vain I Tried to Tell You: Essays in Native American Ethnopoetics.* Philadelphia: University of Pennsylvania Press.

Ives, Edward. 1988. *George Magoon and the Down East Game War.* Urbana: University of Illinois Press.

Ivie, Pamela, and William Schneider. 1978, 1988. "Land Use Values Through Time in the Wainwright Area." North Slope Borough, Barrow, and Anthropology and Historic Preservation, Cooperative Park Studies Unit, Fairbanks.

Iwuji, H. O. M. 1990. "Librarianship and Oral Tradition in Africa." *International Library Review* 22 (March): 53–59.

Jackson, Donald. 1990. *Black Hawk: An Autobiography.* Urbana: University of Illinois Press.

Jackson, Jan Steinbright. 1998. *My Own Trail: Howard Luke.* Fairbanks: Alaska Native Knowledge Network.

Jacobson, Celean. 1997. "A New Freedom for an Old Freedom Fighter." *Sunday Times,* 23 March, City Metro, p. 3.

Kenney, John. 1977. *The Hitchcock Chair.* New York: Potter.

Kingston, Deanna. 1999. "Returning: Twentieth Century Performances of the King Island Wolf Dance." Ph.D. dissertation, Department of Anthropology, University of Alaska Fairbanks.

Kline, Carrie Nobel. 1996. "Giving It Back: Creating Conversations to Interpret Community Oral History." *Oral History Review* 19: 9–39.

Kriger, Ethel. 2001. "Recovering the Silences in the Stories of the Rainbow Nation: The Use of Narrative in the Transformation Process in the National Archives of South Africa." *ESARBICA* 20: 97–104.

Krupa, David, ed. 1996. *The Gospel According to Peter John.* Fairbanks: Alaska Native Knowledge Network.

———. 1999. "Finding the Feather: Peter John and the Reverse Anthropology of the White Man Way." Ph.D. dissertation, Department of Anthropology, University of Wisconsin.

Krupat, Arnold. 1983. "The Indian Autobiography: Origins, Type, and Function." Pp. 261–282 in *Smoothing the Ground: Essays on Native American*

Oral Literature. Edited by Brian Swann. Berkeley: University of California Press.

Kruse, Jack, Michael Baring-Gould, William Schneider, Joseph Gross, Gunner Knapp, and George Sherrod. 1983. "A Description of the Socioeconomics of the North Slope Borough." Technical Report No. 85, Mineral Management Service, Alaska Outer Continental Shelf Region.

Laughlin, William. 1980. *Aleuts: Survivors of the Bering Land Bridge.* New York: Holt, Rinehart and Winston.

Lautaret, Ronald. 1989. *Alaskan Historical Documents Since 1867.* Jefferson: McFarland and Company.

Lee, Christopher. 1999. Review of *The Seed is Mine. Oral History Review* 26 (1): 132–35.

Leighton, Alexander H. and Dorothea Leighton. 1983. "Eskimo Recollections of Their Life Experiences." *Northwest Anthropological Research Notes* 17 (1 and 2): 1–437.

Lomax, Alan. 1975. *The Folk Songs of North America in the English Language.* New York: Doubleday.

Luke, Howard. 2000. "Respect, Gaalee'ya." With Ann Oury Lefavor. Pp. 95–112 in *Under Northern Lights: Writers and Artists View the Alaskan Landscape.* Edited by Frank Soos and Kesler Woodward. Seattle: University of Washington Press.

Lurie, Nancy. 1961. *Mountain Wolf Woman, Sister of Crashing Thunder: The Autobiography of a Winnebago Indian.* Ann Arbor: University of Michigan Press.

Lyster, Richard. 1997. "By Trading Justice for Truth, South Africa Will Rewrite Its History." *The Sunday Independent.* 20 July.

Makhubele, Amos. 1997. "The Story of Little Big Man." Recorded by William Schneider.

Mather, Elsie. 1995. "With a Vision Beyond our Immediate Needs, Oral Traditions in an Age of Literacy." Pp. 13–26 in *When our Words Return: Writing, Hearing, and Remembering Oral Traditions of Alaska and the Yukon.* Edited by Phyllis Morrow and William Schneider. Logan: Utah State University Press.

McClellan, Catharine. 1975. *My Old People Say: An Ethnographic Survey of Southern Yukon Territory.* Part I. National Museums of Canada Publications in Ethnology 6. Ottawa.

McNamara, Katherine. 1986. "Frances Dementieff." Pp. 59–98 in *The Artists behind the Work.* Fairbanks: University of Alaska Museum.

Metayer, Maurice. 1972. *Tales from the Igloo.* Edmonton: Hurtig.

Mercier, Laurie. 2001. *Anaconda: Labor, Community, and Culture in Montana's Smelter City.* Urbana: University of Illinois Press.

Miller, Penny. 1979. *Myths and Legends of Southern Africa.* Cape Town: T. V. Bupin Publications, ABC Press.

Mishler, Craig, ed. 1988 (2001). "The Loon's Necklace: A Native American Tale Type." Paper presented at the annual meeting of the American Anthropological Association, November 1988, revised March 2001.

———. 1995. *Neerihiinjik We Traveled from Place to Place: Johnny Sarah Hàa Googwandak: The Gwich'in Stories of Johnny and Sarah Frank.* Transcription by Judy Erick, Lillian Garnett, and Mary Rose Roberts, with assistance from

Ron Frank, copy editing and tone marking by Katherine Peter and Jeff Leer, song transcriptions by Tony Scott Pearce, family tree by Kenneth Frank and Craig Mishler. Fairbanks: Alaska Native Language Center.

Mitchell, Donald C. 1997. *Sold American: The Story of Alaska Natives and Their Land, 1867–1959.* Hanover: University Press of New England.

Mokgoats'ana, Segothe. n.d. "It Is Herstory Too." Manuscript, in possession of William Schneider, University of Alaska Fairbanks.

Moore, Mabel Roberts. 1933. *Hitchcock Chairs.* Tercentenary Commission of the State of Connecticut, Committee on Historical Publications 15. New Haven: Yale University Press.

Morrow, Phyllis. 1995. "On Shaky Ground: Folklore, Collaboration, and Problematic Outcomes." Pp. 27–51 in *When Our Words Return: Writing, Hearing, and Remembering Oral Traditions of Alaska and the Yukon.* Edited by Phyllis Morrow and William Schneider. Logan: Utah State University Press.

———. n.d. "Self-Conscious Communities: Can Telling Make it So?" in "Communities of Memory," ed. Phyllis Morrow.

Movius, Phyllis. 1999. "Review of video, 'Unravelling the Stories: Quilts as a Reflection of Our Lives'" *Oral History Review* 26 (1): 111–12.

Mphahlele, Es'kia. 1984. *Afrika My Music: An Autobiography, 1957–1983.* Braamfontain (Johannesburg): Raven Press.

Mphahlele, Sentsho Ernest. 1992. "Student Unrest at Black Universities in Southern Africa, with Special Reference to the University of the North, 1960–1990." Ph.D. dissertation, Department of History of Education, University of the North, Sovenga.

Mulcahy, Joanne. 2001. *Birth and Rebirth on an Alaskan Island: The Life of an Alutiiq Healer.* Athens: University of Georgia Press.

Murray, David. 1991. *Forked Tongues.* Bloomington: Indiana University Press.

Nagy, Murielle. 1991a. "Qikiqtaruk (Herschel Island) Cultural Study: Final Report." Presented by the Inuvialuit Social Development Program, Heritage Branch, Government of the Yukon, Whitehorse.

———. 1991b. "Qikiqtaruk (Herschel Island) Cultural Study: Interviews 1–20." Presented by the Inuvialuit Social Development Program, Heritage Branch, Government of the Yukon, Whitehorse.

———. 1994. "Yukon North Slope Inuvialuit Oral History." *Occasional Papers in Yukon History* 1. Whitehorse: Heritage Branch, Government of the Yukon.

Nelson, Richard. 1983a. "Foreword." Pp. 1–2 in *Sitsiy Yugh Noholnik Ts'in': As My Grandfather Told It.* Told by Catherine Attla, transcribed by Eliza Jones, translated by Eliza Jones and Melissa Axelrod. Fairbanks: Yukon-Koyukuk School District and Alaska Native Language Center.

———. 1983b. "A Mirror on Their Lives: Capturing the Human Experience." Pp. 15–36 in *Sharing Alaska's Oral History: Proceedings of the Second Alaskan Oral History Conference,* 26–27 October.

Neuenschwander, John. 1993. *Oral History and the Law.* Revised edition, Albuquerque: Oral History Association.

Newman, Turak. n.d. *One Man's Trail.* Anchorage: Adult Literacy Laboratory.

Okpewho, Isidore. 1992. *African Oral Literature: Backgrounds, Character, and Continuity.* Bloomington: Indiana University Press.

Oral History Collection, Elmer Rasmuson Library, University of Alaska Fairbanks.

Patty, Stanton. 1971. "A Conference with the Tanana Chiefs." *The Alaska Journal* 1 (2): 2–18.

Paulin, Jim. 1999. "King Crab Boat Card Deal Tales of Past." *Anchorage Daily News*, 10 November, F1 and F5.

Perlman, John. 1997. "Small-town Truth Hearings Skirt the Surface of a Well of Suffering." *The Sunday Independent*, 29 June.

Pipher, Mary. 1999. *Another Country: Navigating the Emotional Terrain of Our Elders*. New York: Riverhead Books.

Portelli, Alessandro. 1997. *The Battle of Valle Giulia: Oral History and the Art of Dialogue*. Madison: University of Wisconsin Press.

Potter, Jean. 1973. *The Flying North*. New York: Ballantine.

Renner, Louis L., S. J., and Dorothy Jean Ray. 1979. *Pioneer Missionary to the Bering Strait Eskimos: Bellarmine Lafortune, S.J.* Portland: Binford and Mort for the Alaska Historical Commission.

Riordan, Ann Fienup. 1986. "Nick Charles Sr." In *The Artists behind the Work*. Fairbanks: University of Alaska Museum.

Ritchie, Donald. 1995. *Doing Oral History*. New York: Twayne.

Rogovin, Milton, and Michael Frisch. 1993. *Portraits in Steel*. Ithaca: Cornell University Press.

Rosaldo, Renato. 1995. "Foreword." Pp. xi–xvii in *Hybrid Cultures: Strategies for Entering and Leaving Modernity*, by Néstor Canclini Garcia. Minneapolis: University of Minnesota Press.

———. 1980. "Doing Oral History." *Social Analysis* 4 (September): 89–99.

Rosengarten, Theodore. 1974. *All God's Dangers: The Life of Nate Shaw*. New York: Knopf.

Ruppert, James. 1995. "A Bright Light Ahead of Us: Belle Deacon's stories in English and in Deg Hit'an." Pp. 123–35 in *When Our Words Return: Writing, Hearing, and Remembering Oral Traditions of Alaska and the Yukon*. Edited by Phyllis Morrow and William Schneider. Logan: Utah State University Press.

Sabo, George. 1997. *Communities of Memory: Histories and Reflections on the History, Culture and Life in Nome and the Surrounding Area*. Nome: George Sabo Publisher.

———. 1999. *Communities of Memory II: More Life Stories and Adventures from the People of Nome and the Bering Strait Region*. Nome: George Sabo Publisher.

Sam, Robert. 1998, 1999. "The Cannibal and the Mosquito." Three tellings of the story, the last at the national Oral History Association meetings in Anchorage, Alaska.

Sarris, Greg. 1993. *Keeping Slug Woman Alive*. Berkeley: University of California Press.

Schneider, William. 1976. "Beaver, Alaska, the Story of a Multi-Ethnic Community." Ph.D. dissertation, Bryn Mawr College.

———. 1987. "A Sense of Context and Voice in an Oral Biography." *Northwest Folklore*, 6 (1): 31–38.

———. 1990. "Elders Voices Echo Links to Land." *Fairbanks Daily News-Miner, Heartland Magazine*, 11 February, p. H5.

————. 1995a. "Lessons from Alaska Natives about Oral Tradition and Recordings." Pp. 185–204 in *When Our Words Return: Writing, Hearing, and Remembering Oral Traditions of Alaska and the Yukon.* Edited by Phyllis Morrow and William Schneider. Logan: Utah State University Press.

————. 1995b. "When the Words Keep Pounding in My Ears: A Study in Personal Narratives." *Northern Review* 14 (Summer): 67–85.

————. 1996. "Stories to Heal—Stories to Prepare for the Future." Draft evaluation of the Kotzebue Communities of Memory, 4 April.

————. 1998a. "More Than Words on a Tape: The Problematic in Converting Orality to Material Custody." *South African Archives Journal* 40: 94–100.

————. 1998b. "Ch'eghwetsen' in Story, Song, and Deed: Lessons from Chief Peter John." Paper presented at the annual meeting of the Alaska Anthropology Association, 20 March.

————. 1998c. "Nome and the Power of Story." Paper delivered at the annual meeting of the American Folklore Society, Portland, Oregon, October.

Schneider, William, Kgwerano Isaac Matibhe, and Mlamli Maqoko. 1997. "Public Oral History Records in a Multi-cultural Society." Pp. 50–56 in *The Nature, Identity and Role of Public Archives in Southern and Eastern Africa at the End of the Twentieth Century: Proceedings of the Fourteenth Biennial General Conference of the Eastern and Southern Africa Regional Branch of the International Council on Archives,* Pretoria, 30 July–1 August. Pretoria: National Archives of South Africa.

Schneider, William, Sverre Pedersen, and David Libbey. 1980. *The Barrow-Atqasuk Report: A Study of Land Use Values Through Time.* Occasional Paper 24. Fairbanks and Barrow: Cooperative Park Studies Unit and the North Slope Borough.

Sheppherd, Joseph. 1988. *A Leaf of Honey and the Proverbs of the Rainforest.* London: Bah'ai Publishing Trust.

Sidney, Angela. 1988. "The Story of K̲aax̲'achgóok." *The Northern Review* 2: 9–16.

Skotnes, Andor. 1995. "People's Archives and Oral History in South Africa: A Traveller's Account." *South African Archives Journal* 37: 63–72.

South African Government. 1997. "Batho Pele, White Paper on Transforming Public Service Delivery." General Notice 1459. *Government Gazette* no. 18340 (October).

————. n.d. Department of Provincial and Local Governments, Directorate, Traditional Affairs. The White Paper on Traditional Leadership. (www.polity.org.za/govdocs/discuss/draft-traditonal2.html)

————. 2000. Department of Provisional and Local Governments, Directorate, A Draft Discussion Document: Towards a White Paper on Traditional leadership and Institutions. 11 April.

Stahl, Sandra. 1977. "The Oral Personal Narrative in Its Generic Context." *Fabula: Journal of Folktale Studies* 18: 18–39.

Stanford, Dennis. 1976. *The Walakpa Site, Alaska: Its Place in the Birnirk and Thule Culture.* Washington: Smithsonian Institution Press.

Stayt, Hugh. 1968. *The Bavenda.* Cass Library of African Studies. London: Frank Cass and Co.

Sun, Joe. 1985. "My Life and Other Stories." Translated from Inupiaq by Susie Sun, compiled by David Libbey, funded by NANA Museum of the

Arctic and Alaska Humanities Forum, logistical support provided by
National Park Service. Manuscript. Rasmuson Library, University of
Alaska Fairbanks.

Talayesva, Don. 1942. *Sun Chief: The Autobiography of a Hopi Indian*. Edited by
Leo Simmons. New Haven: Yale University Press.

Tanana Elders. Recording H95-47, tapes 1 and 2, Oral History Collection,
Elmer Rasmuson Library, University of Alaska Fairbanks.

Tarnai, Nancy. 2001. "Natives Gather to Push Mental Health Programs for
Kids." *Fairbanks Daily News-Miner*. 1 April 1 2001, section B1.

Tedlock, Dennis. 1979. "The Analogical Tradition and the Emergence of a
Dialogical Anthropology." *Journal of Anthropological Research* 35 (4):
387–400.

———. 1983. *The Spoken Word and the Work of Interpretation*. Philadelphia:
University of Pennsylvania Press.

———. 1990. "From Voice and Ear to Hand and Eye." *Journal of American
Folklore* 103 (408): 133–56.

Titon, Jeff Todd. 1980. "The Life Story." *Journal of American Folklore* 93
(369): 276–92.

Toelken, Barre. 1996a. *The Dynamics of Folklore*. Logan: Utah State University
Press.

———. 1996b. "From Entertainment to Realization in Navajo Fieldwork."
In *The World Observed, Reflections on the Fieldwork Process*. Edited by Bruce
Jackson and Edward D. Ives. Urbana: University of Illinois Press.

Tonkin, Elizabeth. 1994. *Narrating our Pasts: The Social Construction of Oral
History*. Cambridge: Cambridge University Press.

Trouillot, Michel-Rolph. 1995. *Silencing the Past: Power and the Production of
History*. Boston: Beacon Press.

Trudeau, Gary B. 1987. "Gary Trudeau and the Impertinent Questions: The
Commencement Address." *Smith Alumnae Quarterly* (summer): 4–8.

United States Interagency Arctic Research Policy Committee. 1990.
"Principles for the Conduct of Research in the Arctic." Prepared by the
Social Science Task Force, 28 June, Appendix G, pp. 88–89.

University of Alaska Museum. 1986. *The Artists behind the Work*. Terry Dickey,
project coordinator; Wanda Chin, project designer, and Suzi Jones, guest
curator and editor. Fairbanks: University of Alaska Museum.

Van Onselen, Charles. 1996. *The Seed is Mine: The Life of Kas Maine, A South
African Sharecropper, 1894–1985*. Cape Town: David Philip Publisher.

Warren, Gwendolin Sims. 1997. *Ev'ry Time I Feel the Spirit*. New York: Henry
Holt.

Webster, Helen. 1989. *Inugaq: Bone Game*. Iqaluit: Nunatta Sunaqutangit
Museum Society, Elder's Program, 1987–88, Baffin Divisional Board of
Education.

Wickersham, James. Diary. Wickersham Collection, Alaska State Library,
Juneau

Worl, Rosita, and Charles Smythe. 1986. "Jennie Thlunaut." Pp. 123–46 in
The Artists behind the Work. Fairbanks: University of Alaska Museum.

Index